# Almost Right

## SONYA FERRELL

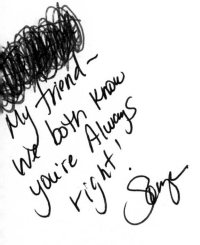

My friend —
We both know
you're Always
right!

This is a work of fiction. Names, characters, places, and incidents either are the product of the author's imagination or are used fictitiously, and any resemblance to actual persons, living or dead, business establishments, events or locales is entirely coincidental.

# DEDICATION

This book is dedicated to Bayliss. Parenting you has been
one of my life's greatest blessings. I love you!

# ACKNOWLEDGMENTS

For my readers who have encouraged me to continue this journey. Thank you for helping me nourish the creative pieces of my soul.
For every person who is blessed to know and love someone whose life path allows them to explore mental health challenges.
For my family, an extra special thank you for your tolerance, patience, love, and support.
For Tonya, thank you for your patience and expertise.
For my dear friend Julie B, the fastest beta reader this side of the swamp, thank you, thank, you, thank you!
For Tiffany, you are amazing and you continue to make me better. I couldn't do this without you, nor would I want to.
For Kenneth, thank you more than I could ever put to paper.

# PROLOGUE

As a mother, you have one job. Be an advocate for your child. With a single cry, babies demand priority over your own parents, your husband, even yourself. It's a job many women look forward to even as children themselves. I was no different. I looked forward to the day I could wear the many hats of motherhood. I wanted to look in a mirror and see a provider, an educator, a protector, and a confidante. I was prepared to succeed, too. When a mother succeeds, society benefits. When she fails, the entire world suffers.

I was under the impression a good mother could also manage to have a good marriage and be a good wife. I never expected to have to choose.

# CHAPTER 1

Sitting behind the wheel of my grey Buick
LaCrosse, I checked my reflection in the visor
mirror for the fourth time. My skin was clear.
There was nothing in my teeth. Not a hair was
out of place in my low, sleek bun. I'd been
sitting in the car for over twenty minutes, so at
this point I was officially procrastinating. I was
afraid of what waited for me inside. Nettie's
transfer to Waterview Mental Health and
Wellness Center last month was the only thing
that could have made me come back here. I
doubted Waterview had changed much in
twenty years. I was certain the things that kept
me away for two decades were still quite
prevalent. I was in no hurry to smell the
disinfected air and hear the shoes squeaking in

2

the hallways leading to rooms that locked from the outside only.

I didn't want to see Nettie in clothes without strings or buttons. I didn't want to see her with a glazed, medicated, empty stare. I didn't want to see her sitting like a lump on a log staring at nothing, but I had already been told to expect just that. Since that awful day at the police station, where Nettie confessed to all those terrible things she believed she'd done, she hadn't said a word. After the detectives determined no crimes had been committed, the police transferred her to the hospital. There, a bunch of tests were run and consultations were done. We were referred to Dr. Ruth Mercier. Her eyes were kind and warm even as she told me things I could barely wrap my mind around. I listened to what she had to say and because it was in Nettie's best interest, I allowed them to bring my sweet girl to this God-forsaken place. All I wanted to do was bring my baby home, but I knew I wouldn't be up to caring for her long term. This was Daniel all over again.

Digging in my purse, I found my lip balm and reapplied it for the umpteenth time. Sitting outside wasting time doing grooming checks was not going to get it. In or out. Stay or go. It was time to move or leave. With a quick prayer, I squared my shoulders and stepped out of the car. The sun shone warmly on my face and I sighed. It never failed to amaze me how the weather could be so perfect in the face of such tragedy. How dare a bird sing when my loves were in a mental health facility?

Just like the small sign near the door, the building was plain and unassuming. Neutral earth tones with shy peaks of blue and green accented a brick and stucco combo. The building was far enough from the main road to mute the sounds of traffic, but close enough to pretend not to be isolated.

A sudden gust of wind lifted the hem of my skirt and tugged strands of hair across my lips. Tucking my face into my shoulder, I strode toward the entrance. Everything was exactly as I remembered. The signage, the door handle, the plants in their beds along the sidewalk, all the same. Squelching the urge to turn tail and run, I opened the door and put one foot in front of the other. As I breached the doorway, the Earth didn't stop turning and the building didn't collapse on my head. Lucky me. Expecting an onslaught of sanitized air, I began breathing shallowly through my mouth. With trembling hands, I signed in and waited to be escorted to my little love.

The pictures on the walls were supposed to inspire tranquility. There were no hard lines. The colors were soft, and the images morphed into whatever you wanted them to be. It was a lot like sitting in a field and cloud watching. If you wanted to see a dog, there was a dog. If you squinted and turned your head a certain way expecting a crab, it magically appeared.

There was no clock on any wall I could see and I was too nervous to dig around in my purse for my phone. I should have prayed more before I came here. I wasn't ready to see Nettie. I wasn't prepared to be this close to Daniel. I'd just about made up my mind to reschedule when my name was called. Swallowing a curse, I followed an aide through an unmarked door.

I was expecting to be taken to one of the nondescript, locked rooms along the hallway, but I was led directly to Dr. Mercier's office and advised she would join me momentarily. I chose to sit in the brown leather chair closest to the door in case I needed to make a hasty exit. Fighting down panic, I briefly wondered if I was going to need to reserve a room for myself. Maybe they would put me between Nettie and Daniel. I felt hysterical laughter bubbling up inside my chest and clapped my hands over my mouth. I knew I was being ridiculous, but given the circumstances, who wouldn't? Deciding it would be too much of a cliché if I came unglued in a shrink's office, I firmly placed my sweaty palms in my lap. I forced myself to take a deep breath and looked for somewhere to focus my mind. I allowed my eyes to skim the room, passing certificates and plaques.

There was a lovely oil painting behind her desk and I chose to see it through what I liked to call my *"art eyes"*. Though I hadn't considered myself an artist for many years, I still found myself considering the world through a creative lens from time to time. On the surface I saw a benign bouquet of tulips. The lines were bold and the colors were vibrant. I loved tulips. Daniel would often bring bunches of them to my office when we were dating. The painting was so well done, it made you want to smell it. Finally calm, I was able to give a genuine smile to Dr. Mercier when she came into the room. I extended my hand to her, but she went for the hug.

It was strange to find myself enveloped in her warm embrace. I hadn't seen her since Nettie's transfer, but she hadn't changed much. She barely came up to my shoulder, but her presence was larger than her stature. It was sort of like being on the receiving end of one of my own hugs. Nervous and embarrassed, I stepped away and settled back into my chair. As I sat back down, part of me wanted to put off the conversation and get another hug, while the rest of me resented the sudden need for comfort through contact.

"Mrs. McCarvey. I'm so glad you decided to come. Please have a seat. I'd like to chat with you before you see Nettie."

I wasn't prepared for a chat. I was expecting a run down on Nettie's medications and the visitation protocols. Do this, don't say that. If this happens, we'll buzz you out of the room. I wasn't trying to be negative, but that's kind of where I was with things. I was already drawn as tight as a bow. I felt as though one more unexpected turn would cause an explosion or disintegration or nuclear holocaust. Slamming the drama door shut, I forced myself to focus and try to take in everything Dr. Mercier had to tell me.

"Mrs. McCarvey, I'm sorry to say there hasn't been much of a change in your daughter. Nettie has not spoken directly to anyone in the ten weeks she's been here.

We've had to dress her, feed her and bathe her. Yesterday was the first time she attempted to attend to any of her personal functions with assistance, so I called you. Even the smallest effort on her part may indicate she wants to come back to us. She is lightly medicated only because she was agitated the first few weeks of her stay here. I imagine, with time, that will change and we will be able to discontinue some of her medications.

"The reason we want you here is so you can talk to her. Hearing your voice may ease her on some level and help her reconnect. I know this is all a new experience for you, but I believe it will make a difference. Don't be surprised if she doesn't respond right away. As I told you before, she can hear you and on some level she is aware of you. She does occasionally make sounds, but we've found they are a response to whatever reality is going on in her head rather than any external stimuli.

"As you know, I watched the video she made at the police station. For two years she'd not only convinced herself of your death, but had fully accepted the blame. Now, we've told her multiple times you are alive and well, but perhaps you'd like to tell her your version of things from when you arrived at her apartment. It's just a suggestion. Are there any questions I can answer for you before you see her?"

Questions? I had plenty of questions. Was this my fault? Was she going to get better? When could I bring her home? Afraid of her answers, I swallowed them and shook my head no. I didn't fully trust my voice. The look on her face told me she wanted to say something else, but I stood abruptly, cutting her off. One can of worms at a time. I had no desire to talk about her 'other patient', period. Her eyes full of compassion, she acknowledged my unspoken answer to her unspoken question with a slight nod. She pushed a button on the phone and the same aide reappeared to bring me to Nettie's room.

The walk through the building was unsettling. I couldn't quite get a feel for where I was in relation to the parking lot, and I wondered if that was intentional. We arrived at a small room near the end of a hallway that looked like every other hallway in the building. I let the aide open the door for me and I stepped inside. The click of the lock behind me was startling. I knew it was coming, and I fought past my panic. This moment wasn't about me. I was here to help heal my child. I was afraid to speak, terrified of saying the wrong thing. I sent up my thousandth silent prayer and sat on the little stool next to her bed.

She was just as I'd envisioned, sitting in baggy nondescript clothes with her feet tucked under her backside looking out the window at nothing. As I looked at her, my heart began to break all over again. I was haunted by thoughts of the 'other patient'. I had to physically shake my head to dislodge the thoughts and images. Now wasn't the time.

Refocusing on Nettie, I took in every detail from her clothes, to her hair, to her hands. Her nails and cuticles were ragged, but her hair was styled in the same sleek bun as mine. I wanted to weep. I wanted to grab her by the shoulders and demand she snap out of it. I wanted to wrap my arms around her and never let go. I did none of those things. Instead, I somehow found my voice and began to speak.

"Sooo… Dr. Mercier advised me to come in here and talk to you. I don't know what I'm supposed to say. I don't know where to start. I'm still surprised to see you alive after all this time. I suppose you may feel the same way. I keep going back and forth between crying and praising God. I never gave up hope. Your room at home is just the same and I packed your apartment. All of your Langston things are in totes in the attic. I refused to throw out a single scrap of paper. I figured at some point you'd want to go through all those things yourself.

"After I got home from the hospital in Oklahoma, I waited to hear from you. I figured you'd run away with your young man, Leonard. A month passed. Then two. The people from the apartment office called to find out why you hadn't paid the rent. It took me two whole months to realize you were missing. Baby, I'm so sorry!

"Of course Grandy and I hurried back to Oklahoma immediately. I extended my leave of absence at the church and filled out a missing persons report. We checked every hospital and morgue in the state. I was so desperate, I even contacted Leonard. Reaching out to him was tough on me. I wanted to be angry with him, but the poor boy was devastated. I know you didn't feel he had any God in him, but he did allow me to pray with him. I guess he was desperate too. For the first few months you were missing, he and I talked daily. Then it was weekly and then it just stopped. I suppose he had to move on. I don't know what the two of you had, but I believe it changed him."

I thought mentioning Leonard would trigger something, but she didn't even look my way. She kept staring out the window at nothing. Unable to keep still, I stood up and began to pace. Walking in a tight circle, I was at a loss for words. I knew this would be hard, but the fear of losing her the way I lost her father was overwhelming. Taking a different approach, I cleared my throat and began again.

"You look so different. You're still my little chocolate china doll, but you've changed. Your face is the same, but your eyes. They're so burned out. So hollow. I've been in here for half an hour and you've barely blinked. You haven't moved. I want to take you in my arms and squeeze the breath out of you, but I don't believe I can bear not getting a hug in return. Dr. Mercier said you can hear me and the more I talk to you, the better you will get. I'm not sure I believe her. Right now I feel like a fool talking to a mannequin.

"I told Grandy I was coming today. He wanted to see you, but Dr. Mercier thinks it may confuse or overwhelm you. He wants me to tell you about your Dad. He said I owe you an explanation and I suppose he has a point. I believe a lot of what's going on with your mental state may have started with your Dad. The thing is, I never wanted to tell you any of that. My life with him was complicated. I don't like thinking about it. It's too hard to look back at how we were at the beginning of our marriage and then come to where things ended up. Who would have thought I'd end up with the two people I loved the most living in the same mental health facility?

"As much as I hate to admit it, Grandy may have a point. We decided when you were born not to involve that side of the family in our lives. In fact, it was his idea. Now we realize what a mistake that was. I should have told you about Daniel a long time ago. He was and still is the love of my life. It's been years since I've seen him, but I think about him every single day. I think about how we met. I think about our marriage. I cry a lot for the happiness we shared and I cry for the life we could have had.

"To tell you the whole story, I'd have to explain my life before your dad. This all started with your grandfather and my mother. Just like you and I never talked about your father, Grandy and I had a hard time talking about my mother. It was and still is a touchy subject. Honestly, I don't want to focus too much on how things were with Grandy back then. If he was sitting here, he wouldn't want to either. He and I had so much ugliness back then. We put our differences aside when you came along, but deep issues like ours don't just vanish on their own.

"It wasn't always easy growing up with your grandfather. He was driven by things I could never see. All he did was work, go to church, and harass me. I barely recognize the marijuana smoking conspiracy theorist who laughed and joked with you. The man I remember was hard, unsmiling, and rigid. I never doubted his love for me, but he was heartbroken over my mother and determined to make me the perfect image of everything she wasn't.

"I guess the best thing to do here is to jump right in, but not tonight. I don't want to come in here and blurt a bunch of things that may or may not help. Dr. Mercier says I should journal my thoughts and write things about our visits so you can read them when you feel up to it. She also said writing will help me sort and organize my thoughts. I hope so, because right now my brain feels like scrambled eggs. I'll be back tomorrow evening after work. I love you, baby."

I waited for some sort of acknowledgement, but she never moved. Feeling more uncertain than ever, I stood to leave. I wanted to touch her, hold her, smell her, but I didn't dare. For some reason I felt as though I no longer had the right. Our last real conversation wasn't exactly pleasant. I wondered if mine was even a voice she wanted to hear. Instead of reaching out, I forced myself to push the buzzer. As the latch clicked open I hated myself for leaving, but staying was not an option.

# CHAPTER 2

Back in the safety of my car, I completely fell apart. I cried so hard I made myself sick. I sat for what felt like forever crying until my throat was raw and my eyes were almost swollen shut. I knew I should have tried to focus on the positives, but how? I wanted to pray, but how? I had nothing good to say to the Lord in that moment and I was terrified. I needed to go home, but I didn't want to take a chance on Papi seeing me. I knew how awful I looked. I certainly didn't need any witnesses to my meltdown.

To kill time and get my head together, I went to the malt shop and ordered a shake. I drove around aimlessly for two hours. Times like these made me miss Daniel so much. I was so tired of dealing with everything by myself. Just once I would have liked to let him comfort me about something dealing with Nettie. With a resigned sigh, I closed the door on that train of thought. It was never going to happen. It was close to nine by the time I pulled into the drive. All of the lights were out except the one over the stove, so I knew Papi was already in bed. I was glad. Tomorrow I was going to delve into a lot of pain and misery, a great bit of which I could lay at his feet. I wasn't interested in looking at him just yet.

I went to my room and settled at my desk. Time to write or journal or whatever. I wasn't sure how it was going to help, but at this point, I didn't see where it would hurt. I felt a little silly, so I decided if all of this was supposed to be for Nettie to read, I may as well approach it like I was writing a letter to her.

*Dear Nettie,*

*I really enjoyed seeing you this afternoon. I wish you would have spoken to me, but I understand if you're not ready to talk. I was content to do all the talking anyway. When I was driving home, it occurred to me that I never talked to you enough growing up.*

*Our communication was perfunctory. Logistical. Where are you going? When do you need it? What are you doing?*

*I was so busy trying to make a good life for you and be a good mother, I managed to repeat every mistake your grandfather ever made with me. I was so determined to be a perfect mother, I ended up turning your childhood into a perfect mess. You must have thought I was completely out of touch with all my quaint little sayings. Well, I got those silly things from your grandfather. Why I decided to pass them on to you, I'll never know! They didn't do me any good, and they probably did even less for you.*

*Your Grandy had this saying. He started almost every lecture I can remember with it.*

*"Almost right is always wrong. How many times do I have to tell you this, mon Angel?"*

*That was his personal mantra and I suppose on some level, it became mine as well. I bet you can't imagine your Grandy giving me a stern lecture, but it happened so often, I could almost recite them. One of them sticks with me for some reason.*

*I remember sitting on my small padded stool at*

Papi's feet, staring morosely at his boots. They looked fine to me. Better than fine, actually. They weren't new, but I could see my reflection in their tips. I knew better than to ask where the imaginary scuff was. There was nothing to do but start over. Schooling my expression, I remember squaring my shoulders, and preparing for the lecture. Reorganizing my supplies, I focused on perfect boot polishing, emptying my mind of all distractions. Tucking two fingers around a fresh cotton ball, I began making small circles near the sole of his right boot. If I didn't get it together, I was bound to be polishing until daylight. As it was, Papi was starting the long version of 'the lecture'.

"Vivianne, your mother was a beautiful woman. I wanted to marry her the first time I heard her laugh. It sounded like a tinkling bell and I felt her laughter from my nose to my toes. She was tall and trim. She minded her figure. She was a good cook and kept a clean house. She was demure in public. She put on a good show. That's how she got me! Looks can be deceiving, Vivianne. On the surface everything was proper, fine and well, but at home when it was just the two of us she was a wild woman. Always laughing and singing out loud. Letting her hair fall into her face. It was disgraceful. At times I was afraid she'd forget herself and act out in public the way she did at home. Some days I wish she'd never sashayed her way into my store!

*At a glance and on the surface of the thing, she was perfect for me, but almost right is always wrong."*

*I'd heard all this before. Papi worked their story into his lectures at every opportunity. I knew most of his version of their brief marriage by heart. I used to listen attentively, hoping for new details. Sometimes as he was winding down, his voice would become wistful. I was so hungry for the tiny morsels of my missing mother, the lectures were almost worth it. Unfortunately, the older I got, the more bitter his tone became. After a while, it felt as though he'd reached a point where he seemed angry they'd ever met. I used to wonder if eventually he would be angry at me for existing. If that had been the case, we would have been on the same page. During my late teens, I felt the same way.*

*I knew he didn't say those things to be cruel or make me feel bad. In his mind he was protecting me. He didn't want me to turn out like her. It couldn't have been easy to run a business, raise a child, and be active in the community as a single man. True, he was single by choice, but the why of things changed nothing. He was very clear about what he expected from me. Righteous perfection. A daughter whose character was above reproach. A young lady whose reputation would always stand up to public scrutiny. If I was brave, I could have saved us both a bunch of trouble. I knew deep inside, I was more her than him. A lot more.*

*It was no big secret I was the spitting image of my mother. Papi was a normal, average looking man of medium build, height, and complexion. As a teenager, I was as exotic as my mother was reported to have been. Tall and light skinned with long hair, I had her high cheek bones and almond shaped eyes. My voice was hers as well. In grammar school I'd been embarrassed about the husky timber of my voice, but I grew into it. By the time I graduated from college, I realized it was captivating. What I previously deemed husky or masculine was actually sultry and seductive.*

*The majority of what I knew about my mother was hearsay. No one talked to me directly about her. From time to time I'd overhear people talking to each other behind their hands just in earshot. Everyone in town knew someone that either knew her or knew of her. She had quite the reputation. None of it was bad, exactly. To the little town of Lampling, Louisiana, her uniqueness was juicy. She was not bad, but she wasn't good either. She was different during a time when different was scary. They said she laughed at everything and everyone, and she sang radio music. Everything about her was bigger than life. She was more. Taller than most men, lighter skinned than her family members, longer hair than the ladies at church, prettier than the women she passed on the street.*

*Her family moved around a lot and at some point she landed in Lampling. The word gypsy was tossed around but I preferred to think of her as some type of exotic butterfly. In my mind she would flit from one beautiful thing to another, spreading happiness and smiles. It was easier to paint her with a saint's brush than to believe she just abandoned her family on a whim. Beauty can't be caged and fair or not, I thought of Papi as her cage.*

*I heard these things about her and I would say to myself, "I sing radio music, too. I just do it in my head to keep down confusion. I want to laugh out loud at nothing, but I wouldn't want to upset Papi. I would love to let my hair blow in the wind, but Papi would find it distasteful."*

*If Mama really did run away from his cage, I only fault her for not taking me with her. Sometimes I was all about the mystery of Helene. Why? Where was she now? Was she sorry she left us? Was she even still alive? Why did I even care?*

*Then I would consider Papi. As much as people liked to gossip about Mama, the same folks loved talking about Papi. He was like some sort of legend in our community. He owned a small grocery store in the center of town that was patronized by both Black and White customers equally. As sad as it is to say, back then, that fact alone made him notable. He was Chairman of the Deacon Board at church and taught Sunday school as well. He was a Tuskegee graduate with a degree in business and had served briefly in the Army. The people in Lampling were very proud to have produced such an upstanding citizen.*

*That was all well and good, but all those accolades had a flip side. In my experience, the only thing people in small towns took more pride in than the success of a native son would be his downfall. The whole point of placing people on a pedestal in small towns like ours was to knock them down. That was where my mother came into play.*

*Her name was Helene Dubois. I don't know if she deliberately sought out my father. I don't know if she came into his store looking for a husband. From what I've been told, he took one look at her and was immediately smitten. By all accounts, she spoke and he was dumbstruck. There was something lyrical about her voice. He had always been so focused and driven, no one could remember him dating anyone special before my mother, but everyone remembered their courtship. It* was so short it was scandalous. He asked her father if she could come to a church picnic with him. She packed thick ham sandwiches wrapped in wax paper, fresh fruit and pickle spears. They sat under a tree and talked so much, they forgot to eat. After that date, they were seen together every day. He proposed and they married within six months of meeting. There were conversations about if there would be a "premature" baby, but that was not the case. I was born just over ten months to the day after the wedding, a honeymoon baby. Mama was nineteen and Papi was twenty-nine.

They should have been happy, but in Lampling there is no such thing. Papi worked harder than ever in the store after I was born. He wanted to turn his store into a legacy to leave me and any future children who came along. Longer hours meant less time for picnics. Papi expected my mother to cook, clean, and keep house. She was to be seen and not heard, existing for his comfort only. He would come home to a hot meal, a beautiful wife, and a clean quiet child. He would share details about his day, telling her who came into the store and what had been purchased. For a while she was fine with living to please and listen and comfort, but she got bored. She needed to go and see and do for herself.

When I was about one, she started bringing his

*lunch to the store instead of packing it ahead of time. She'd make a big production of unpacking each item and his fifteen minute lunch breaks started taking forty-five minutes. The customers that came in would begin talking to her and visiting with me. Her laughter brought a crowd and the ladies started hanging around the store, bags of purchased goods in hand, laughing along with her about everything and nothing. Husbands started complaining to him about the amount of time and money their wives spent at the store, so he banned her from bringing lunch. A lot of women would have gotten angry, but my mother acquiesced and went back to staying home.*

*A year later, her need for adult conversation drove her to join the choir, but that was an unmitigated disaster. First, she was not always available when Papi come home from work. His dinner would be on a warming plate in the oven, and he was coming home to an empty house. Instead of coming home directly after rehearsal, my mother would stay and talk to the musician or some of the other ladies. The hour she should have been gone regularly turned into three. The other problem was her voice. Since she sang the same way she spoke, everything she sang sounded seductive and secular. When people heard her sing, they felt like she was singing only to them and there was some sort of intimate secret they were sharing. Papi pitched a fit, so* she resigned her position and tried to be a happy homemaker again.

The following spring, she decided she needed a hobby. One afternoon, she packed me up and drove to Alexandria to buy a bunch of art supplies. She had no real plan about what to create, but she longed to make herself into something more than Helene the wife and Helene the mother. She bought clay, paint, canvases, sketch pads, smocks and two little French berets, one for me and one for herself. I vaguely remember the trip because going to Alexandria meant a frozen ice for me if I behaved. We were only gone for a few hours, but Papi heard about it in less than one. From what I heard, he was livid.

People have said he completely lost his temper. The yelling began before she could unpack a single bag from the car. The neighbors could hear him screaming and throwing things. There was name calling and door slamming. They say the only voice they heard was his. My mother never said a word. This went on for hours. At some point it was quiet and then it was morning. The word was Papi's rage wore itself out and he fell asleep in his chair in the family room by the front door.

When he woke up the next morning, she was gone.

*It hurts more than I thought it would to put that on paper, but there it is. She left us. Helene's departure seems like a sour place to leave a letter, but it's almost midnight and I still have work in the morning. Just know that even as I tell you these things, I love you. They aren't being brought up to cause pain. I suppose by me getting this type of history out in the open, you can have a better sense of yourself and of me. Anyway, that's all for tonight.*

*Love,*

*Mama*

# CHAPTER 3

Feeling foolish about the letter, I wasn't sure what to do with it once it was finished. The secretary in me demanded it be sealed in an envelope, so I did. I wasn't convinced she would ever read it, but I decided to drop it off on my way to the church in the morning.

I wasn't tired, sleepy, or hungry, and putting all that ancient history on paper woke something inside my mind that refused to go back to sleep. I stood up and grabbed my hairbrush. A habit born years and years ago when sleep and peace were out of reach, I sat at my vanity and brushed my hair. I wasn't sure what needed to be written and what needed to be told. Some things were probably necessary for me to share, but surely some parts of the story would be mine and mine alone at the end of all this.

Somehow I was going to have to bring myself to talk about my mother and my husband -two subjects had been off limits for decades. Those doors had been closed and sealed with good reason. I had always known Daniel would come up eventually, but the mother talk was a surprise. It had been a long time since I'd given this much mental energy to her. The bottom line for me was she left. What was I supposed to add to that?

With her gone, I became Papi's whole world. Even though I was only four at the time, when she left, I knew something was terribly wrong. My Mama was missing. There was no music. No laughter. No color. There was also no crying. Everything was muted. Papi worked even more and I was left to manage my feelings on my own. I had so many questions. Did he ever talk to her? Did she leave a note? Where was her family? Did he know where she went?

For a long time he ignored my questions. For years he changed the subject when I asked about her. When I reached puberty, it changed. After years of never mentioning her, one night he decided to tell it all. He sat me down and told me his version of their story for the first time. Before that night, the only time he mentioned her was in *the lecture*.

I thought I was ready for his talk. In my mind, I'd created a fantasy mother. Actually there were multiple fantasies. In my favorite one, she would walk into the store one afternoon. She'd apologize for leaving me, throw her arms around me and beg me to forgive her. Of course I would, and we'd hold hands as we went to the house to reunite the family. Papi would be overcome with emotion because he never meant to push her away. They'd mend their fences and I'd get my family back. The end!

After years of hearsay and conjecture, I was finally going to have a complete picture of the two people I held the closest. There had to be a happy medium in this story. There was no way my mother could be the villain because I felt myself becoming her. She was always with me. I looked in the mirror and she was there. Could I magically stop being her daughter? Could I make myself more him and less her? Lately, when I spoke, my voice had become hers. I know that must have been hard for Papi, but what could be done about it?

Papi couldn't be the villain because he'd

done nothing for the past ten years but pour into me. Teach me. Mold me. He was stern and hard, but I recognized it was love and fear that drove him. I overheard him praying one night. He prayed for me, not for himself. Both of my parents were equally wrong, but whatever had been done must have been for loving me.

I sat a cup of tea in front of him and grabbed a cup for myself. I didn't dare interrupt with any questions. I was afraid he would stop. He spoke for two hours straight. He laughed a few times and smiled a bit at the beginning, but by the time he got to the end, his jaw was hard and set in an ugly way. His version of things was worse than anything I could have imagined. He painted her with a terrible brush. I was devastated. The part that hurt the most was the abandonment. The way Papi explained things, she was flighty, selfish and irresponsible.

I was fourteen years old and that day I made a solemn vow. I promised myself I would never ask about Helene again. She was now Helene, never Mama again. She left me. She left *us.* Firmly placing myself in charge of keeping Papi happy I threw everything I had into being the opposite of all I knew my mother to be. I cooked, cleaned, studied, and prayed. I suppressed my laughs, and became a more muted me.

When I was not at home, school or church, I was at Papi's elbow in the store. I learned how stock, clean, advertise, and organize. Papi had given up on having more children, but my dedication to his store showed him there would be a legacy to pass on. What I failed to realize at the time was the only person capable of making him happy was staring at him in the mirror each morning. I'd given myself an impossible task.

After our talk, I got very serious about school. I stopped socializing and became a people watching bookworm. I separated myself from my classmates and focused on school, work, and church. The kids thought I was being snooty, but I didn't care. I spoke when spoken to, did my work, and spent every free moment in the store. I tried not to think about Helene, but from time to time she popped into my stream of thought. On the rare occasion I laughed aloud, she was there. I had her laugh. When I glimpsed myself in the mirror before bed, with my hair down we were twins.

When I turned seventeen, my connection

to her became stronger. It was quite by accident. Papi was in Baton Rouge for a church conference and I decided to use the time alone to straighten up in the attic. Usually I never went up there. Twenty minutes in, I saw three brown paper bags. They looked out of place because everything else up there was boxed and labeled. The bags were in a far corner behind Papi's old Army trunks. Before I even opened the bags, I knew who they belonged to. Until that day, I'd never seen anything in the house that belonged to Helene.

Picking them up, I opened them one by one. Looking inside those bags did something to me. The façade of calm organized dedication to Papi cracked a little. All of my righteous anger with Helene morphed into a longing. For the first time in years, I wanted to talk to her. I'd heard Lampling's version of my parents. I'd heard Papi's version. Suddenly I was interested in her side of things.

Afraid of my emotions, I put everything back the way I'd found it. I wanted to tell Papi about Helene's bags, but I didn't. Knowing about them was my secret. I couldn't stop knowing or stop seeing and somehow my discovery unmuted me. I wasn't as disconnected after that. Suddenly I wanted connections, laughter, noise. Anything would be better than wading though someone else's expectations of my life.

For years I'd watched my peers develop real lives all around me. On the outside, I was uninterested. I didn't care about their dances and dates, their fun. On the inside, for the first time in my life, I envied them. I longed to dance and sing. I knew the popular music, but I didn't dare let their lyrics pass my lips. The most I could bring myself to do was hum occasionally, and I felt guilty about that. I remember realizing maybe small pieces of the life I lived in my mind could be reality. Suddenly I was eager to go to college and see what the world beyond Lampling had to offer.

Feeling a bit more settled, I put my brush back on the vanity. Remembering my optimism about leaving for college allowed me to get ready for bed without feeling choked with sadness. I was glad Dr. Mercier suggested the writing thing. The idea of talking to Nettie about being abandoned by one parent and pressured to the point of breaking by the other one was less than appealing. Nettie would read the letter or she wouldn't. I decided to let her deal with it at her own pace. She was alive and well and safe which was more than I could say this time last year.

With a sigh, I sank to my knees at the side of my bed and prayed. For the first time in a long time, I felt good about my conversation with God. I'd been struggling with my prayer life since I realized how sick Nettie was. I was glad she'd been returned to me, but I was frustrated because once again, I was forced to deal with something I didn't want to acknowledge. Seeing her video was like being in those last days with Daniel all over again. It wasn't fair.

After seeing her and doing the writing thing, I felt my attitude shifting. Maybe this was a good thing. Maybe I would be able to help her in ways I couldn't help her father all those years ago. As I slid between the sheets, I had a new purpose. I was surprised to find myself looking forward to talking to Nettie again. I realized she probably wouldn't speak to me, but suddenly I was eager to share my memories of college and of her father with her.

# CHAPTER 4

Going to see Nettie after work was on my mind the entire day. I woke up, prayed, and made a pot of coffee for Papi and a cup of tea for myself. For the first time in a long while I realized I wasn't harboring any secret animosity toward him. I thought, if putting things on paper made me feel this good, it was going to become a daily thing. I left home early enough to drop the letter with the receptionist at Waterview, then went to work feeling uplifted and optimistic.

After I left my office, I went directly to Waterview. I was in a hurry to sign in and see my girl. I was slightly disappointed to find her in almost the exact same spot, but I pushed the feeling aside and told myself to remember all the things Dr. Mercier said about unfair expectations. Clearing my throat, I sat on the little stool at her bedside and began to speak.

"Nettie, I wrote a letter to you after I left last night. I hope you got a chance to read it. Today I want to tell you about my college days. This morning I thought about all of your Oklahoma boxes. It got me thinking about when I left home for the first time. I know you thought I would be terrified to let you go all the way to Oklahoma for college.

"The truth was, I wanted you to leave. I needed you to get away. I hoped you would find your true self there because that's where I found my own truth. In college, I stopped being Gerald Fontenot's daughter. No one knew about the store. No one cared that my mother ran off. No one minded that I looked like her. I became my own version of Vivianne, partly because of the college environment, and partly because of your Dad.

"Leaving to attend college was the most exciting thing I had ever done. I knew Papi was proud of me for leaving and anxious for me to get my degree and come back home. His plan was for me to take over the store and maybe expand into Alexandria. He had my entire life planned including college and marriage. He didn't realize I was on to him. It made him happy to plot and it made me happy not to argue. I found it was easier to just let him have his fantasy daughter. Why not? I had my own fantasy life. Neither of our visions for my life was likely to come true so it didn't matter either way.

"When I packed to leave, I debated about whether or not to bring Helene's shopping bags with me. I had no plans for the stuff in them. As a matter of fact, I'd only opened them once. At the last minute I decided to bring them with me and they ended up on a shelf in the back of my closet. They stayed there for the first two years of school.

"One day my roommate Paulette asked about them. She and I had become somewhat close, so I gave her the short version about their contents and about my parents brief marriage. I'll never forget her response. Her words changed my life. She said, 'Girl, your mother didn't buy all that stuff so it could get shoved to the back of a closet shelf somewhere. I imagine she planned on using it and you should do the same.'

"Until that moment, I'd kept those bags as some kind of secret shrine. These were the only things I owned that my mother picked up, examined and chose. I was in awe of them and I was intimidated by them. Paulette was right. When it came down to doling out advice, she usually was. After she left the apartment that day, I took the bags down and sat them on my bed. I took my time examining each item.

"I opened the first bag. It had eight little jars of paint, several different little canvases, two table easels, and a sketch pad in it. I opened a few of the jars and found the paint reduced to a tar-like consistency. Setting the paint aside, I picked up one of the canvases. Even though I handled it carefully it felt taut and brittle. I fought the urge to throw it all away. I kept the easels and sketch pad and put the rest of the things back in the bag.

"The smallest bag held paint brushes, pens, pencils, chalk, and erasers. I put them with the sketch pad and easels and turned my attention to the last bag. I didn't have to open it. I'd only seen the contents once, but I knew them by heart. Two smocks. Two berets. Two balls of clay wrapped in plastic.

"The last bag always confounded me. How could my mother plan to create with me, and then leave me behind? She never said goodbye. I'd never taken the items from the last bag before, but for some reason, that day I was compelled to. With trembling hands, I put on my mother's smock and beret. I looked at myself in the mirror and imagined I looked a lot like she would have looked when she left. Turning my head this way and that, I studied my profile. I pouted, I smiled, and I frowned. Looking at my face and seeing hers was unsettling, to say the least. I looked exactly like I remembered her. I couldn't handle that thought so I turned back to the balls of clay.

"I unwrapped one of them and was surprised to find it still moist after so many years. It was cool to the touch and smelled like dirt. I couldn't stop playing with it. I tore off a piece and rolled it around between my palms. I made a ball, then squished it. I reformed the ball then made another one. I stacked the balls and added more. Soon my mindless creation took the shape of a person. The little clay doll made me smile, so I made another one. Then a third. Without thinking, I'd created a family. My family. I started to smash them, but instead, I went into the kitchen and grabbed a few toothpicks. Using them I began to make details in my little doll family. They became distinct in their features. The father stern, the mother laughing, the child in play.

"I etched and smoothed and sculpted for

hours, working on the little family I wished I'd had. When Paulette came back, she knocked on my door and parked herself at the foot of my bed. She looked at the little family and went nuts. She acted as though she'd never seen anything so beautiful. She really made a fuss. I was embarrassed and proud. Once I stopped working on them and really looked at them, I understood. I couldn't get over how life-like they were. Uncured, unpainted, they appeared ready to move on their own if you gave them a chance.

"The next day after class we took them to an art studio off campus to see about curing them. The lady there had the same reaction Paulette had the day before. She offered to buy them, but something in me rebelled at the idea of parting with my little family. I looked at the mother and thought giving her away would be like losing my own mother all over again. Instead, I offered to make new one for her. If the realistic little family I'd created was born of love and longing, there was plenty more where that came from.

"Making those dolls for her was the beginning of an unexpected career. For the past two years, I'd been feeling like a cog in Papi's machine, destined to get the degree he picked, work at the store he created, marry a man he selected, and live a life he chose. I'd been dressing for his approval, laughing in my mind and being a good little marionette. Suddenly it was as though the strings that moved me were finally meeting a little resistance. The doll that thought she was alive and allowing the string pulling had decided to stop playing along.

"It's easy to go along with someone else's plan for your life as long as you don't have a plan of your own. With the sale of that first figurine, my plan for my life was born. I didn't know it, but there it was. At that time, at that time I felt the universe placed me on a path to become an artist.

"Nettie, I know my art was something I hid from you, but I had my reasons. My art, my business, and the sculpting represented things I felt were lost to me when I moved back to Louisiana. I slid back into a version of myself that I felt I could use to protect my sanity and raise you properly.

"I did research, refined my technique and let my hands do their thing. Before long I was making enough money selling my figurines to pay my own rent as well as my tuition. I was afraid to tell Papi, so I let him continue to send me money. I kept up with my school work and continued to excel in my classes, but my joy came from creating. I felt alive when I sculpted.

"There was a large part of me that wanted to call Papi and tell him about my work, but on some level deep inside I knew telling was a bad idea. I never knew exactly what he'd said to Helene to drive her away, but I had no desire to hear it firsthand. I could never endure hearing words so cruel they would make me abandon not one, but two people I loved. I kept my secret for two years, thinking about her the whole time."

Standing suddenly, I realized I'd been talking for over an hour. My back was starting to get stiff and my mouth was dry. I felt raw and wrung out. I thought the revelation of my secret career would elicit at least a glance, but I didn't get a grunt or a sigh. I was pouring my heart out, dredging up some of the most important things in my life and Nettie was looking out the window.

"Nettie, Baby this really is hard to do, you know? I want to keep talking to you, but coming here is going to be hard on me. Bringing this stuff back up is like reliving it all over again. I wish you would at least look at me or acknowledge me and let me know you hear me. I really do love you. You have to know that much. I'll be back tomorrow. I'm not going to stop coming until you tell me to. Plus, I guess saying these things and writing about them helps me too. I love you, baby."

# CHAPTER 5

After I signed out, I realized once again I wasn't ready to go home. The next thing I needed to tell Nettie was how I ended up living in Florida. That meant sifting through the wreckage of the emotional earthquake that almost killed my relationship with her beloved Grandy. I was getting zero feedback from her so I wasn't completely convinced telling her these things was helpful. I wanted to ask Dr. Mercier for advice, but I wasn't interested in being psychoanalyzed. I didn't need a doctor to tell me I had abandonment issues and mommy issues and daddy issues.

Looking around I realized I was near our church. On impulse I decided to stop in. When she was younger, Nettie always liked hanging out in the sanctuary and playing in the patterns of stained glass on the carpet. I liked being there when it was quiet and dark. Using my work keys, I let myself in, walked to the sanctuary, and sat on the first row of pews.

There was a beautiful mural behind the pulpit that was illuminated at all times. It was a depiction of the healing of the woman with the issue of blood. In it she was on her knees with her hand extended toward Jesus. Whenever I looked at it I was reminded of another Papi-ism. *Faith plus effort equals results.* That woman had to press and try to get to Jesus.

Thinking back, I remember making the decision to stay in Florida. After one of my trips home, I realized avoiding Papi's manipulation was impossible. He thought he knew so much about me, but he failed to recognize that I'd changed. Being away from Lampling allowed me to grow into the woman I would never have become if I'd stayed. For the first time in my life I was willing to cut my mother some slack. I knew why she had to leave. I still thought there was a better way for her to have handled it, but I got it.

I graduated with my business degree in 1973. I knew I had to come clean about my plans. There was no way I was going to give up the financial liberation and joy I received from my art. Going back to Lampling to live Papi's dreams was no longer an option. I never intended to wait so long to bring it up, but it wasn't in my nature to be confrontational. I decided to talk to him over dinner after graduation. That way we'd be in public and there would be less of a scene.

Looking at the empty pews around me, I tried to imagine what would have happened if I had just gone with the flow. I could have come home to Lampling, gotten married, raised a family and lived the life Papi wanted for me. Thinking back to the night before the wheels fell off, I was so optimistic.

I remember sitting in front of my mirror brushing my hair with my eyes closed. I was surrounded by the boxes I'd packed with pride and excitement. I was afraid to talk to Papi, but strangely, I was looking forward to it, too. I planned my announcement and reviewed each potential point of contention. I'd secured a job in the dean's office to provide regular income to go along with my art income. I knew Papi wouldn't accept art as a viable career, so staying at the Dean's office would make sense to him. He had no idea how lucrative the art field had become for me, and I didn't think telling him would help my case.

I'd signed a lease on my new apartment, my car was paid in full, and I had a church family. The only obstacle to me staying was him wanting me to leave. Feeling like all my bases were covered, I sighed, content with my plan of action. I actually slept well the night before graduation.

The next morning, I got up, said my prayers, and made coffee. Normally I would have had tea, but somehow I knew I'd need the extra fortitude. Papi wasn't due to come into town until ten and graduation started at noon. I figured we'd zip over to have lunch somewhere before the ceremony so he wouldn't see all the packed boxes and jump to the wrong conclusion. The peace I felt that morning was just the quiet before the storm. The day that should have marked the beginning of so many wonderful things turned out to be one of the worst days of my life.

I hadn't been home to see Papi since Thanksgiving. Usually when I went to Lampling, I took care to dress conservatively and to wear my hair pulled back away from my face. Paulette called it my country Louisiana look. It didn't occur to me to change my look in Florida. It should have. I knew I'd made a mistake as soon as he got out of his car.

Back then Papi drove an old black Cadillac. It was time for a newer model, but he wasn't having it. He didn't like change, and boy did I know it! He got out of the car, stretched, looked over at me and frowned. It was too late to do anything about my clothes, as most of the 'Louisiana' clothes were packed. I started to raise a hand to my hair, when I realized the passenger door was opening. Carl! I couldn't believe he brought Carl.

Papi had been pushing Carl down my throat since before I left for college. He hired him the summer before I moved to help out while I was away. I trained him, but it was not a great experience for me. Carl was a leech. He spent so much time wagging his eyebrows up and down at me, I wondered if he practiced that dumb maneuver in the mirror at home. Maybe he thought he was Groucho Marx. Corny moves aside, there was no attraction for him on my part at all.

At five nine, he was an inch and a half shorter than I was. His body shape was round even though he wasn't overweight. He had a flat pie-shaped face and saggy jowls. He insisted on wearing a pencil thin mustache with a sparse mess he called a goatee. His hair was wavy and fine and he kept it slicked to his scalp. He wore Old Spice and too much of it. He wasn't much for brushing his teeth, but loved mouthwash.

I'm sure he looked good on paper to your grandfather, but to any woman with two eyes, he was just gross. He reminded me of Eddie Haskell from that old show '*Leave It to Beaver*'. He spent more time looking at my breasts and backside than he did listening to what I had to say.

The only time he behaved himself was when Papi was in the store. He never touched me or anything, he just made tacky references to things he'd like to do. He went to the same church we did, so when I was home, I saw him throughout the week. During church I usually sat in front of Papi, and Carl started sitting with him. The idea of having him behind me bothered me so much, I almost joined the usher board just to have an excuse to move. Not having to see Carl was an extra incentive to do well in college.

At Papi's insistence we went on one date. I'd come home for a short visit and I let Papi bully me into going into Alexandria to see a movie with Carl. It was exactly the kind of disaster I thought it would be. He picked me up in plenty enough time to catch the start of the show, but instead of going straight to the theater, he took some long back woods way to get there. Then the fool pulled over to the side of the road and started trying to kiss me.

He said he knew I wanted him since the first time we worked together in the store. He tried to slide his hand under my sweater and stuck his tongue in my mouth. I literally gagged. Bile pushed into my throat and there was no help for any of it. I threw up. He shoved me away and threw up too. So my first kiss was pretty much the worst thing that could have possibly happened. We were both covered in vomit so instead of going the movie, he had to bring me home. Anyone with sense would have let that be the end of it, but Carl felt like he had something to prove, so he kept trying. After a point, I just stopped coming home all together.

The last time I went home, Carl proposed. I knew Papi had put him up to it. Instead of just saying no, I asked him if he knew my middle name. Rather than answer me, he looked toward Papi. Ugh! I wanted to be a sass mouth and ask him if he expected Papi to come on the honeymoon, too, but I didn't want him to twist my sarcasm into a yes.

Before he started working in the store Carl and I had only spoken a handful of times since graduating from high school. We didn't have friends in common, similar hobbies, or even the same taste in music. I knew he was interested in me only because Papi sold him some big dreams about owning a chain of grocery stores.

Seeing him stroll toward me cool as you please made me mad enough to cuss out loud. Him being at my graduation promised to complicate an already complicated day. There was no way I was going to tell Papi about my decision to stay in Florida with Carl around. Even though it was the last thing I wanted to do, I was going to have to go back to Lampling, even if it was only for the weekend.

After the ceremony I went back to my apartment and unpacked a few Lampling clothes to put in a suitcase. Next to my bed, my little family stared at me from the nightstand. Those figurines were very close to my heart. Looking at them, it seemed as though they knew how I felt in that moment and what I was thinking. Don't go! Don't go! On an impulse I grabbed them and brought them with me. Maybe they would give me the strength to say what needed to be said. God knew I would need courage when I finally made my case.

I insisted Carl ride back with Papi. That wasn't what they wanted but I didn't care. There was no way I was getting into a car with him again. I didn't make a big production about the travel arrangements and I knew Papi, like me would never argue in public. It was a six hour drive from Florida to Lampling, so it was well after midnight by the time we made it home. I was exhausted. All I wanted to do was grab a quick shower, brush my hair and crash. What ended up happening was just the opposite.

As soon as Papi came in to the house, he began an absolute tirade. He went ballistic. In my entire life, he'd never yelled at me. Not even once. I was expecting a difficult conversation, not a conniption fit.

How dare I disrespect Carl? How could I embarrass them like that? Who did I think I was? I let this go on for about ten minutes. Obviously he needed to get things off his chest. I figured I'd let him say his piece, retreat to my room for the night and try to sort things out in the morning. I let him rage until he hit a nerve. He brought up the money he'd been sending and for some reason it set me off like a rocket.

He said, "How dare you waste my money at that fancy college? I didn't send you there so you could sashay around with your hair all in your face and wear hippie clothes! I should have made you come home two years ago. Carl has been waiting for you to get your degree, but I told him it wasn't going to make a difference. After the babies come, you're going to need to be at home anyway. It doesn't take a degree to raise children. You're going to end up just like your mother!"

That did it. All the way home, I'd been building myself up to share my plans for my life. I'd talked to Paulette about it and she used the word 'marionette' in her response. I couldn't shake the word. She was right again. Papi had been pulling my strings from the time he told me about Helene leaving us. It was time to separate myself from their failed marriage and live the life I chose for myself.

Turning away from him, I went to my room and opened my suitcase, grabbed the little family and an envelope. I calmly walked back to him and placed everything on the coffee table. Looking into his eyes, I chose my words carefully. I wanted to make sure he understood how serious I was and what I had to say was about more than that moment.

"Papi, I love you so much, but I'm not moving back to Lampling. I will never marry Carl. The perfect daughter doesn't exist. The sooner you wrap your head around that, the happier you will be. I'm not Helene. I'm like her, but I'm me. I'm more like my mother than you will ever know, and I'm not going to apologize for it or hide it anymore. I will never stop loving you, but I am done with you controlling me. As for your money, it's all in the envelope. I've made more money in the last two years than you have. Take the money or leave it. I'm going back to Florida."

I didn't wait for him to go to bed and I didn't bother to repack my bags. I snatched up my purse and keys and just like Helene, I left.

I was so upset. I drove all the way to Baton Rouge before my anger waned. As I was driving, I couldn't help but wonder if Helene had traveled this very road fueled by pain and frustration. I wondered what she'd been thinking as the miles took her farther and farther away from me. Did she think about turning back? I did.

I hated to treat him the same way she did, but for the first time I was in her shoes. I got it. Papi had become a manipulative tyrant. If I went back on any terms other than my own, he won. I thought we'd take a break and come back together after a few months. The reality was we didn't speak again for more than twenty years.

When I left Lampling, I never tried to reconcile with Papi. I really believed he would call or show up or send a letter. When he didn't, I wouldn't. I missed him, but I refused to be the one to give in. When months turned into years, I knew I should have reached out, but I didn't know how. The bad news was our broken relationship. The blessing was me meeting Daniel.

Shaking myself free of the memories, I looked again at the beautiful mural. Again I was blessed with feelings of calm and purpose. Faith and effort were good, but prayer was a necessary part of the woman's equation. With that thought in mind, I sank to my knees for a much needed talk with the Lord. I prayed for peace in my heart as I continued to delve into painful memories and I prayed for God to give me the right words to explain things I still didn't understand myself.

Finished with my prayer, I stood, locked the church and headed home. The plan was for me to go home, write Nettie, shower, and get some sleep. I felt the peace I'd asked for and I felt sure the words I needed were coming. While all of these things would be news to Nettie, I knew the story by heart. It had happy moments, but overall, it was harsh. I wanted her to understand even the most beautiful diamond is born from Earth's crushing pressure. Bad things sometimes gave birth to marvels.

# CHAPTER 6

*Dear Nettie,*

*I have been debating how to bring your father into my talks with you. All the other conversations have been appetizers and fillers. My dealing with Daniel represents the meat of what I need to say to you. I should have told you about your Dad years ago. It's just that our relationship was so intense. So adult. There are some things a woman should keep to herself. I also feel that if I don't tell it all, you won't really understand things. The passion and the fire I shared with Daniel equally represent what was so right and what was so wrong about us. I guess what I need you to take away from this is how much we loved each other.*

*I know from Oklahoma, that you are no stranger*

*to what goes on between a man and a woman when they care a great deal for each other. Walking in on you and Leonard in bed was quite a shock. It was the first time I realized that despite my coddling, meddling, over protective behavior, you'd managed to grow up. I'd never perceived you as an adult until that moment. The way you defended your relationship to me that morning made me see you in a new way. You made your love for him very clear. Please know it was the same for Daniel and I. Your relationship with Leonard and my relationship with Daniel had more in common than you may think. For my own reasons, I felt the need to keep him a secret from your grandfather, just as you kept Leonard from me.*

*Over the years, I wanted to tell you different things, but I felt I couldn't pick and choose. I thought if I opened the door, I'd have to tell it all. I wanted you to know only the good things and protect you from the rest, but I knew you would never be content with part of the story. How was I going to tell you things I could barely face myself? I spoke to Paulette this afternoon and as usual she put it very plainly to me. She said, "Girl, why do you think you get to choose what is good and what is bad? There is no good Daniel and bad Daniel. It's just Daniel. All of it. Nettie looks in the mirror and sees Daniel just as sure as you can see Helene in your own reflection. You may as well give it to her straight, just like your Daddy should have done for you. With her imagination, there's no telling what kind of father she's created in her mind all because you're too much of a chicken to own your shit!"*

*Well tomorrow, I'm going to sit down, look you in the eye, and own my 'shit'. Whether it makes a difference in you or not, we'll see, but at least the truth will finally be told. Goodnight Sweet Girl.*

*Love,*

*Mama.*

With that settled in my mind, I sealed the envelope, placed it in my purse to drop off on my way to work, and slid between the sheets. I waited for sleep to take me, but my thoughts were chasing themselves around in my brain. Resting my hand on my stomach my mind wandered to the last time I saw Daniel. As usual when I wandered down that particular road, my stomach began to clench and cramp. I broke into a sweat. My lungs felt like they were full of water and my throat was full of sand. I felt my emotions spinning out of control and I couldn't make it stop. It was like my brain had picked up a hot poker and couldn't put it down. After more than twenty years, it was the same. Sitting up in bed, I made a conscious effort to take ten deep breaths. Counting them slowly, I felt the tangles in my stomach ease. By the time I got to eight, my hands stopped shaking. At least this time, I wasn't crying. My panic attacks were fewer and farther between, but they had been vicious for many years.

When I first moved back, I'd take off in the middle of the night needing to escape myself, but having nowhere to run. I'd drive out into the woods, sit in my car and just scream. My eyes would burn with unshed tears and my skin would crawl with the memory of the itch of dried blood between my fingers.

I wasn't in the mood to think about that night and I forced myself to focus on something else. My thoughts landed on Helene, another taboo topic. I hadn't thought about her this much in years. Of course I wondered about her off and on as Nettie and I passed certain milestones, but that was another door I tried to keep shut. My mother's absence in my life was always such a raw spot. Sometimes I wished she was around to tell me what to do with Nettie, but then I reminded myself, she wouldn't know. Desperate for sleep, I tried counting sheep, but big surprise, that didn't work. I finally drifted off around midnight, but my dreams were terrible.

I saw Helene and Papi standing at the edge of a cliff. She was falling. Their arms were extended toward each other, but I couldn't tell if he had pushed her or if he was trying to catch her. Her mouth was stretched open in a voiceless scream. I saw myself standing in mid-air, ankle deep in a cloud. I was close enough to see, but too far away to help. Looking into her terrified eyes, they slowly became my own. Suddenly I was the one falling. Looking up, I could see my parents, Nettie and Daniel. I fell forever and the bottom never came.

Forcing myself awake, I didn't need an interpreter to know what the dream was about. Ready or not my issues were going to be dealt with. It was time. Looking at the clock, I confirmed it was too early for me to be awake. Part of me wanted to go see Nettie, but what good would that do? I planned to broach the big topic of how her dad and I connected and I wanted to be completely honest. I'd spent the last twenty years slamming that door shut, boarding it with nails and blocking it with furniture. Now because there was no other choice, I was taking down the barricade one piece at a time.

Frustrated once again with the no sleep scenario, I decided to get a head start on my day. I took longer in the shower than I normally would have. I shampooed and shaved, thinking all the while about how to bring Daniel into Nettie's world. I'd spent more than twenty years refusing to acknowledge his existence, just to find myself having to serve his memory up on a silver platter.

Our relationship had been full of love and laughter. The good in him was better than good, but the dark side of Daniel was almost beyond comprehension. I had no desire to paint her dad as a monster. He was the love of my life and he nearly destroyed my soul. After all these years, I was still madly in love with him. Not a day went by without me praying for him and as much as I loved him, I never wanted to see him again.

The only way I could deal with this was directly. Anything else would be unfair to Nettie. Sending up another prayer request for fortitude, I got out of the shower, toweled off and got dressed. Papi's door was still closed, so I set the coffee pot to auto start, grabbed my purse and headed to work. It was going to be a long day.

# CHAPTER 7

I dropped Nettie's letter off and drove to work with a heavy heart. I couldn't shake the dream. My lack of sleep bit me in the behind constantly, but somehow I made it. During lunch, I contemplated taking an extended break and going to see her, but I talked myself out of it. Instead, I called Paulette and chatted about nonsense to pass the time. I'm sure she knew how unsettled I was feeling, but rather than call me on it, she allowed me to ramble on about superficial nothingness. By the time we got off the phone, my anxiety was mostly gone and I handled the rest of my day without incident.

On the drive to Waterview, I focused on remembering Daniel as he was when we met. I didn't want to allow any wounds to color Nettie's introduction to him. As poorly as things turned out, at the beginning, we had no reason to think we wouldn't have our happily ever after. Love was still a pretty, shiny thing and I wanted to share that with her. As I signed in, I realized I was almost eager to delve into my love for Daniel for a change. Walking to her room, I sent a silent prayer asking God to give me right words to say.

She was at her perch, looking out the window. I wanted to sit next to her, but I was afraid of spooking her. She looked the same as she did when I left last night. My fear was that she would never come back to me. I tried to follow her unblinking gaze, but from where I stood, I didn't see anything that would warrant her undivided attention. With a sigh, I took my place on the little stool and cleared my throat. Not sure where to start, I clasped my hands together, closed my eyes and began to speak.

"Nettie, today I'd like to tell you how I met your Dad. After the big blow up with your Grandy, I never expected to have anyone in my life. My only example of marriage was his tainted mess. I had no reliable references for relationship building as many of my friends, co-workers and acquaintances were on second and third marriages. I decided to be content with church, work and art, keeping most people at arm's length.

"I loved working in the Dean's office and I loved my art work. Occasionally I'd go to dinner or theater with friends from college, but as they married, moved away, or had kids, I let the friendships fade. I maintained my connection with Paulette and with Holly, my art broker. I bought a house on the beach with big picture windows and settled into a routine that comforted me. Before I knew it, it was 1991 and the world had almost passed me by. I was a thirty-nine year old virgin who lived alone and only had one kiss. The only thing missing was a bunch of cats.

"I didn't want to put effort into dating, but I didn't want to be alone. The idea of a marriage turning out like my parents' made me reluctant to put myself into the dating pool. I resisted any matchmaking. I felt like if the Lord wanted me with someone, he'd bring him to my doorstep. Funny, but that's pretty much how I met your Dad. Daniel changed my life. With him, there was no routine. It wasn't love at first sight, but my response to him was visceral. He came into my office one afternoon looking for Dean Jackson.

"Dean Jackson dealt with all of the discipline issues on campus. He had a reputation for being stern and humorless. Most of the students who came in to see him had a certain look about them. They were nervous or defiant or apologetic. Daniel didn't fall into any of these categories. He came across as jubilant or jovial. He was clearly in trouble for something or else he wouldn't have been there. Strangely enough, he carried himself as though he was there to meet a good acquaintance for a shoo-in job interview. He walked up to my desk, extended his hand and introduced himself.

"Hello, Ma'am. My name is Daniel McCarvey and I have a two o'clock appointment with the Dean."

"I was startled by his introduction, his manners, and his voice. I looked up from my papers expecting to see Teddy Pendergrass standing in front of me. He wasn't, but what I saw instead was better than anything Hollywood or Motown could have ever conjured. The first thing my brain registered was tall. Your Dad literally towered over my desk. I couldn't resist the urge to stand up. Still holding his hand, I stood abruptly and realized that even with me at my full height, he was five inches taller than I was.

"He was wearing a crisp, blue, collared shirt. The top button was undone and it was tucked into a pressed pair of black slacks. I tried and failed not to notice how lean his stomach and hips were. He caught me staring. I should have been embarrassed, but I wasn't. My reaction to him was completely foreign. I quickly took in every detail about him. His skin was so black and smooth it shone like ebony. I smelled cologne, but it wasn't overpowering. It enticed me. I wanted to lean into him. I almost did, but I suddenly remembered myself. When our eyes met, it seemed to startle us both.

"Mr. McCarvey, I believe he's expecting you. You can have a seat over there," I told him.

"At the sound of my voice, he jumped. I was used to people telling me my voice didn't match my face. I often apologized for it, but I didn't this time. The look on his face made me want to keep talking. No one had ever looked at me that way before. His eyes said he wanted to touch me to see if I was real. His mouth said he wanted to eat me because I was delectable. My heart was going ninety to nothing and my legs threatened to give way if I didn't sit down. Shaken to my core, I settled myself back into my desk and tried to refocus on the papers in front of me.

"I was shocked to realize for the first time in my life I was attracted to someone. I wasn't sure I liked it, but I was powerless to stop it. I found myself wanting to check my hair and clothes. I was suddenly ravenous for information about him. As soon as he was called back, I looked in his file.

"He was in trouble. It figured. I'd waited almost forty years to meet a man I was attracted to, and he was everything a father would want his daughter to avoid. The Daddy issues continued. Refocusing on his file, I frowned. Providence United was a Christian college and had very particular rules in place regarding behavior both on and off campus. I'd picked Providence because it was close to the beach. As beautiful as I found lakes and bayous, I'd always wanted to experience sunsets on the beach. At first I'd worried about Papi getting on board with me going so far away, but the rigid behavior expectations were one of the main selling points for Papi. He was opposed to me going to LSU even though it was much closer because there were too many opportunities for me to be 'led astray'.

"According to an anonymous complaint,

Daniel was seen in a piano bar singing and drinking. That was completely against the rules. This was his first time in to see Dean Jackson, but these were things that would probably get him expelled. He may as well have burned a Bible on the chancellor's desk. According to his information, his major was music. He'd finished his bachelor's degree and was almost done with his masters. He still lived on campus and until recently he'd been a member of the campus choir. It was too bad. He was young, handsome, and probably talented. Doing a bit of quick math, I figured he was only twenty-four. Well out of my range.

"I remember sighing and turning my attention back to work. I tried to pretend not to be curious about what was going on in the next office. I decided not to look up when the door opened. Typing away, I closed my eyes as his cologne wafted past me again. I recognized it. Cool Water by Davidoff.

"When I opened my eyes he was gone, but there was a card on my desk. It was his phone number. I didn't know whether to be flattered or insulted. I tucked the card into the side of my purse and tried to finish the last few papers in front of me.

"When I got home that evening, I went

straight for my sketch pad. It had been a long time since I'd drawn anything for my own pleasure. My pencil seemed to have a life of its own. I drew Daniel in detail, my fingers flying over the page. He was beautiful. I couldn't stop visualizing his dark skin. I mentally revisited his grip and his smell. His black eyes reminded me of an onyx ring Papi used to wear. His lips were full, his jaw strong. If I was ever going to have a man in my life, I wouldn't be mad if he looked like Daniel.

"Smiling to myself, I looked at what my hands had created. I realized I'd been humming and I didn't care. I had an overwhelming urge to call Paulette, but that was silly. First, I hadn't talked to her in almost a month. Second, what was I supposed to say? I knew Daniel's name, I had his number, but what else? I wasn't sure I was going to call him and I wouldn't know what to say to him if I did. I felt like a teenage girl with my first crush. Content to let it keep, I put my sketch pad away, turned to my nightly routine and grabbed my hairbrush. To call or not to call? Paulette or Daniel?

"I went to bed grinning and woke up the same way. The next day was Saturday and I spent the morning in my studio sculpting.

During that time most of my work was special order. People would submit photographs of their loved ones and I'd breathe life into what I saw turning the photos into perfectly sculpted miniatures. I had orders to complete. I was supposed to be working on a group of sisters as a surprise for their parents, but my hands refused to obey.

"They made Daniel over and over again. I had a general idea about his overall build, but I may have taken a few liberties. I couldn't get over his towering height or the breadth of his shoulders. I kept thinking about how warm, firm, and strong his grip was. I really wanted to shake his hand again. I made him over and over in various poses. Smiling, laughing, singing. Of course I would have been embarrassed if I thought there was any way for him to find out what I'd been up to, so imagine my surprise when he rang my doorbell just as I was stopping for lunch.

"Feeling guilty I jumped away from my worktable and threw a damp cloth over my little Daniels. I seldom had any company so I wasn't used to hearing my doorbell. I opened the door and there stood your father, looking and smelling just as good as I remembered.

Remembering molding him that way still

made me blush, so many years later and I found myself inundated with the same feelings of excitement and restlessness. I stood and began to walk in meandering circles between Nettie's bed and the door. With a sad smile, resumed my story.

"Nettie, I've been struggling with how much of this to share with you. It's so much harder to say these things than I thought it would be. I want you to have a good idea about how we came together, then apart, but I certainly don't want to cross the TMI line. Dating your father was the most incredible ride I've ever been on. He was charming, spontaneous, and passionate. Looking back over my life, the months we had together represent the period during which I felt the most alive. I've never used drugs, but with him I felt high. He was intoxicating and addicting.

"When he showed up on my doorstep, it never occurred to me to turn him away. It's as though on some level, I was expecting him. My mind and body suffered a temporary disconnect and instinct took over. Until that moment, I thought I'd live and die alone and disconnected. The possibility of sharing my life with another person on my terms was extremely unlikely. I didn't want to be with a man who'd been married or who'd already had kids. I wanted someone like me and at my age, the pickings were slim.

"I'd decided to be content with a career that centered on creativity. The desire to touch people and make physical connections had been satisfied in clay up to that point. The fact that I'd spent the entire morning molding my version of Daniel's arms and legs was not missed by my subconscious. I knew the clay was a poor substitute for the warmth of human flesh.

"With my heart thundering in my chest, I invited him in. He settled himself on the couch, and again I was struck by how comfortable he seemed. He acted like he'd been in my home hundreds of times and would be there hundreds more. Stranger than that, as I rarely entertained, I should have been uneasy with him there. On the contrary I felt a sense of completeness. Glancing over my shoulder, I shook my head. When I bought that couch, my biggest plans for it involved popcorn, wine, and a fluffy blanket. Seeing a sexy Black man sitting there with his ankle across his knee wasn't a consideration.

"Not willing to examine my lack of panic, I went into the kitchen to start a kettle for tea. I didn't realize he'd followed me until I felt his hand on my hip. Pulling me close, he leaned into me. Again I was drunk on the smell of him as his voice rumbled in my ear."

"Vivi, I had to see you again. I found you last night and I waited until I couldn't stand it anymore. When I heard your voice yesterday, I knew in my spirit I'd just met my wife. Marry me."

"Can you believe that? A million things ran though my mind between the time he touched me and the time he spoke. A marriage proposal wasn't one of them. I wanted to laugh, but somewhere in my soul, I knew he was serious and I knew at some point the answer to his question was going to be yes. Clearing my throat, my voice huskier than normal, I turned to face him. Still in the cradle of his arms, I looked into his eyes and almost lost myself."

"Not today, Mr. McCarvey. By the way, my name is Vivianne and you may have a seat in the living room while I finish making tea," I told him.

He shook his head and smiled at me. "I bet your father calls you Vivianne. To me you are Vivi. Sexy, vibrant, Vivi. I didn't come here for tea. I came for you."

"Nettie, the intensity of that moment was insane. Reaching around me, he turned the stove off and moved the kettle to another eye. He grabbed my hand and pulled me back toward the living room. I knew I should have protested to being man handled, but my will was not my own. Compelled to find out what he wanted, I let him lead me back to the couch. We sat together at an angle, knee to knee. He looked into my eyes and for a moment, it seemed as though he was content to stare. Unsure what to do or say, I stared back. Everything I saw the day before was there again. His full lips, his dark eyes, his broad shoulders. When he finally spoke, I almost jumped out of my skin."

"I'm serious about marrying you Vivi," he said. "But first I'm going to date you. Today I'll take you to lunch in the park and this evening we will go to the beach to watch the sunset. We are going to sit on a blanket and you are going to tell me everything you can about yourself. Then I will tell you all about myself. We are going to laugh and talk and maybe hold hands. Later when the moon gets high enough, we will dance at the shoreline and let the waves lick our toes."

"That was his plan and that's exactly what

happened. Cue the irony. My first date with your father was a picnic in the park. I wondered briefly if what I was feeling was the same kind of magic that drew my parents together. If so, it was strong and not to be denied. Getting into his car, I considered the fact no one knew we were together. It should have frightened me, but instead I was exhilarated. Suddenly I felt Helene inside my mind. Her laughter welled inside me and my smile was so wide, my cheeks hid my eyes. I let my window down so the wind could whip though my hair. Daniel looked over at me, laughed and turned the radio up as loud as it would go.

"For weeks, every date we had was just like that. It was a constant whirlwind of activity, laughter, and emotion. The only peace I got was when he was in class and I was at work. Dean Jackson hadn't expelled him. I guess his charm wasn't limited to me. He was on probation for one semester and as playful as he could be, he seemed to take finishing school seriously.

"One of his classes was gospel music composition. He loved writing and singing. Your Dad was at turns playful and carefree and single minded and focused. On the weekends, he'd come over with his keyboard and play and write while I sculpted. We wouldn't say anything to each other for hours. I loved it. At first I was afraid he'd become a distraction, but nothing could have been further from the truth. I loved having him around. I thrived in his presence and some of my best work was done when we were together.

"As time passed, I began to wonder about his marriage proposal. We'd been dating for nearly a year and things were going great. We'd only kissed a handful of times and I both cherished and feared his touch. I was ready to take things to the next level, but I didn't know how. We started going to church together as soon as we began seeing each other and I knew I wasn't the only one expecting to hear wedding bells. During the Christmas break, we went to Ohio to meet his father. That was terrifying because, like everything else with Daniel, he just sprung it on me. He didn't mention his mother and I was afraid to ask.

"By the way Nettie, yes, it has occurred to me I should have asked a lot more questions where your dad was concerned. His father was very kind to me and went out of his way to make me feel welcome. No one ever mentioned his mother, and considering my own absent mother and my lack of a relationship with my father, I kept my questions to myself.

"The acceptance I felt from Mr. McCarvey made me want to be a permanent part of their family, but I kept my longing to myself. I watched the interaction between father and son and wondered if Papi and I would have enjoyed a different relationship had I been born male. I wasn't jealous, just hungry for that level of acceptance.

"On our last night with his dad, I noticed Daniel had been curiously quiet during dinner. His father carried most of the conversation and I could tell where Daniel got his talent for animated story telling. As I began to clear away the remnants of our meal, your father stepped behind me and placed his hand on my hip. I loved it when he did that. He reached around me and put the plate I was holding back on the table. My breath caught in my throat as he spun me around. Heat flooded my face as he kissed me for what felt like the first time in weeks.

"Your father was always careful to respect my physical and sexual boundaries. Neither one of us was interested in starting something we weren't ready to finish. Because our kisses were so few and far between, my response was always swift and passionate. Just as I was beginning to worry about being caught making out like a teenager, he stepped away. Looking down at me with tears in his eyes, he put a hand to the side of my face and said what I'd been waiting a lifetime to hear.

"I'll never forget a single word he said. 'My sweet Vivianne. I love you with my whole heart. Vivi, I need you in my life forever. I imagined this very moment the first time I heard your voice. In that instant I knew I'd met my wife. You may wonder why I'm not down on one knee, but believe me, I've been on my knees every day and night since we met, praying to God He would bless me by binding your life to mine. Make me the happiest man in the entire world. Help me spend my days making music and my nights making love. Take my name. Give me babies and love me for the rest of my life. Marry me.'

"My body began to tremble and tears spilled onto my cheeks. That was exactly the type of proposal I'd secretly wanted my entire life. I was terrified, excited and in a state of disbelief. I'd come to Ohio itching for a ring, but I hadn't gotten my hopes up. I'd stopped praying for love when I turned thirty. I gave up on marriage after Paulette's third divorce. This was more than I could have dreamed and as he looked into my eyes, waiting for an answer, I found myself wanting to sing and shout, but at the same time speechless. By the time I found my voice, it came out as a throaty croak.

"Yes, yes, a thousand times yes.

"His father came around the corner with glasses of champagne. So basically, that's how things were with your dad. Good. Things were very good. We loved, laughed, and began to knit a life together. I wish we could have stayed that way, but it wasn't meant to be.

"That's enough for tonight, Nettie. I don't want to overwhelm you and frankly I would like to leave it here for a bit. I haven't thought about that night in a long time, but it seems I haven't forgotten a single detail. You know, if you have any questions, you can just jump in any time. I know I wasn't exactly receptive to questions in the past, but we're literally in a different place now, aren't we? Even though things went off the rails with your dad, it is important to me you know how much we loved each other. I'm going to go out on a limb and guess you're still not talking. Well, that's fine. I'll be back tomorrow. I love you, Nettie."

Pushing myself to my feet, I pushed the buzzer and was immediately let out of the room. The aide told me Dr. Mercier wanted to know if I could stop by her office before I signed out. I didn't want to. I wasn't sure what she wanted, but I had a darned good guess. I wondered how long I would be able to keep coming here to see Nettie before someone would decide I needed to see Daniel, too. I didn't have the strength tonight. There was no way. Begging off, I made a hasty exit. By the time I got to my car, I was running like the hounds of hell were on my heels.

Jamming the keys into the ignition, I barely stopped myself from peeling out of the parking lot. I'd avoided seeing Daniel for over twenty years. I knew the time would eventually come for me to see him again, but it was going to be on my terms. Reliving his proposal brought me back to that night and stirred so many feelings. Things I'd buried deep were beginning to resurface. Somehow I doubted a cheesecake milk shake was going to soothe my battered emotions tonight. Turning toward the highway, I headed home to think and pray.

# CHAPTER 8

The drive from Waterview gave me time to think and try to sort my feelings. I decided that even though I wasn't ready to deal with my past as it concerned Daniel, a real talk with Papi was long overdue. So many years ago, I came home with my tail between my legs. Married, pregnant and scared, at the time, I felt I had nowhere to turn. Prepared to face his wrath and terrified of being turned away, I didn't call first. Back then, just like tonight, I sat in the driveway with my hands at ten and two on the steering wheel. My eyes closed and quiet fervent prayers passing my lips. Then, like tonight, I prayed for mercy, understanding, strength, and guidance. I didn't want to dig up bones, but some things should never have been buried in the first place.

Gathering my purse, my work case, and my courage, I forced myself to get out of the car. It was still early enough for Papi to be up, but late enough that he would already have eaten dinner. He was sitting in his recliner with an ashtray resting on his knee rolling the last quarter of an unlit blunt between his fingers. The ashtray was one Nettie made when she was in kindergarten. It still blew my mind he smoked at all. Usually he put all his marijuana and paraphernalia away before I got home, but these days what was usual? The look on his face said two things. First, he knew I'd been avoiding him and second, he wasn't having any more of it.

Resigned, I settled into the matching chair just to his left and waited. Taking his sweet time to talk was something I knew he enjoyed about aging. He liked to start conversations by saying things like, "Well, I probably shouldn't say this, but I'm old so I can say what I please." If the expression on his face was any indication, he'd been working on this speech all day. It looked as though I'd avoided a crappy situation with Dr. Mercier and traded it for another. Willing myself to stay put, I looked around the room. Nothing much had changed in the front room since I was a child, with one exception.

The pictures on the mantle spoke volumes. I never bothered them. They had always been Papi's project. He was very particular about the pictures, the frames, and their placement. There were always four pictures. No more, no less. The changes he made were meaningful, but only to him. As I waited for the lecture to begin, I took note of the current arrangement. There had been a change. I saw my senior portrait, Nettie's, and a picture of Daniel. This morning when I left, there was a picture of Papi standing in front of his old store. This evening, it had been replaced with a wedding portrait. The frame was plain but the couple in the picture was anything but. Though I'd never seen the picture before, I didn't have to get out of my seat to know who they were.

The bride looked just like me. Her dress was simple, but she was intensely beautiful. Even though the picture was black and white, she looked vibrant and animated. It was almost like she could come out of the frame and into the room if she wanted to. I was entranced by her beauty and confused. Where had he kept this picture all these years? The bigger surprise was Papi. He looked so handsome. He was happy and proud. The picture had been taken in front of the house. I recognized the columns on the porch. Only their hands were touching, but there was electricity between them. There was no way he would have been able to keep looking at their picture after she left. I was surprised he hadn't torn it to pieces. I was so overwhelmed by the love pouring from the two of them, it hurt me to look at it.

Turning my attention back to Papi, I realized he'd been watching my reaction to the portrait. He rolled his blunt back and forth between his fingers, but he didn't light it. Though I was full of questions, I held my tongue. He was only going to speak when he was ready and he was only going to tell me what he wanted me to know.

"Vivianne, I never thanked you for coming back to me. Having you here with the baby gave me a chance to do better as a man and as a father. I thought you didn't need the words and I considered our silent truce enough. I was wrong to hang you for your mother's shortcomings and I was wrong to shove Carl onto you. I apologize. I know we probably need to talk about Helene, but we won't. I'm old and I don't have to do what I don't want to. I'm going to bed. I left red beans for you."

And as Paulette would say, "And that's how the cow chewed the cabbage." I was dumbstruck. Where to start? The picture or the apology? I shouldn't have been surprised that he didn't mention the picture. The apology was probably more for him than for me. As I watched him shuffle off to his bedroom, I saw the truth. He was old. With all the turmoil over the past two years, he'd aged without me noticing. His slow and steady steps were now just slow. His once proud and erect posture was stooped. His Sunday cane was now a daily accessory. What was grey was now gone. I wondered if he would get to see Nettie before something medical happened and took him away from us.

He and Nettie shared a special bond. When I came home from the hospital with her, it was obvious he'd decided to parent her in ways he'd never parented me. At the time I was so wrapped up in my Daniel mess, I let him. From the very beginning, he was the one who got up with her in the middle of the night. He bathed her, fed her and read to her. When we went to church, she sat with him. He took her to school and picked her up. They were friends.

It hurt him deeply when I showed him the

video from the police station. He held himself responsible because she talked herself out of turning to him when she first started getting wound up. He also blamed himself for advising me not to bring her father into her life. I think he was secretly afraid Daniel would recover and usurp his position as the man in Netties life.

It never occurred to me to expect an apology from Papi about Carl or the blow up over Helene. I was just grateful for his shelter and support. By the time I came home, he'd sold the store and retired. His time was spent at church, on his porch, or in his recliner. He had friends I didn't know and hobbies I was unfamiliar with. I didn't recognize the man he'd become in my absence, but I was content to coexist with the kinder, gentler Gerald Fontenot.

Because he stayed home with Nettie, I was able to get a job. I accepted a full time position as the pastor's personal assistant and began putting the pieces of my life back together. I stopped taking miniature orders, sold my house, and turned my back on my Florida life. Lampling had grown almost as big as Alexandria and I allowed myself to be swallowed up in my old community.

After I heard his bedroom door close, I stood and walked over to the mantle to examine their picture more closely. Helene held a dainty bouquet with what looked like sweet peas, baby's breath, and daisies. She wore a half veil over her face and her dress came to her mid calf. Even through the veil her eyes seemed to dance and laugh. Her smile was small, showing no teeth, but her jubilance bled through. Papi looked happier than I could ever remember seeing him. I wanted to take their picture into my room, but I didn't.

Red beans didn't appeal to me so I boiled an egg and made toast. Nettie called it my little old lady dinner. I missed her so much. I wanted to see her again, but not at Waterview. I needed her to come home. Thinking about her, I remembered Dr. Mercier's request to see me. It occurred to me I could be wrong about her wanting to talk about Daniel, but I doubted it.

For the past few nights, he had been a constant presence in my dreams for obvious reasons. I saw him as he was when we met and I saw him as I imagined he must look after all these years. For no reason I wondered if he would still smell like Cool Water. Shaking my head at the useless thoughts, I decided to do something to get him out of my process. If I was writing letters to Nettie she may never read, why couldn't I do the same thing for Daniel?

Resolved, I cleared my dinner and went to my writing desk. I had so much to tell him, I didn't know where to start. Truthfully, there was a lot he didn't know. The last time he saw me, I was seven months along with either a boy or a girl. Our marriage had been both difficult and wonderful in the year before the pregnancy. Things had gone from terrific to terrible in very short order. Finding out we were expecting gave us a brief lift before a horrific crash. I never took the time to be angry at him. I just wanted to survive.

Sighing before my blank page, I realized now wasn't the time to write. I wasn't ready rip a Band-Aid off a bunch of bad memories when I still had good things to share with Nettie about Daniel. Instead of writing, I took my shower, brushed my hair, said my prayers and waited for sleep to come. I wasn't going to avoid the clinic and miss talking to Nettie just to avoid Dr. Mercier. Tomorrow, Nettie and I would visit a wonderful time in my life.

## CHAPTER 9

After another fitful night, I was more than ready to go to work. It was no surprise I'd spent the night dreaming about Daniel again. I kept reliving our wedding night and I was exhausted both emotionally and physically by the time the alarm began to blare.

Dressing with care, I decided the worse I felt, the better I planned to dress. I pulled out a pearl colored blouse to wear with a red pants suit. Red wasn't a color I'd normally wear to work, but I'd read somewhere that red was a power color. I decided I could use a little power push. I made sure Papi had a light breakfast to eat with his morning medicine and left before he could comment on my outfit.

On my way to work, I usually kept the radio off. I used the time to make mental to-do lists and organize my thoughts each day. Today

I needed some uplifting. I felt like music so I popped my Tamela Mann CD in. I almost never sang aloud, but as the songs played my heart swelled. I started out humming, but as "Take Me to the King" began to play, I couldn't resist. Not only did I sing, I sang loudly and from the depths of my heart. My spirit began to soar as I worshiped through song. The lyrics were a balm to my battered spirit.

I could feel my attitude shifting. I'd been feeling out of sorts since Nettie was found, but today, thinking about my wedding and my first year of marriage put me in a good place. Working at the church was a bit like getting to go to worship every day. By the time I made it into my assigned parking space I felt uplifted. Despite how things turned out, Daniel loved me and he made sure I knew it. Today I planned to make sure Nettie knew it, too.

When I got to the office I was greeted by the aroma of brewing tea. Rev. Harvey was standing by my desk and my favorite mug was filled. I had no doubt when I took a sip, it would taste of lavender and honey, just the way I liked it. After so many years, he knew me very well. I knew people wondered and speculated about our relationship, but we were more like sister and brother than potential lovers.

A few years back he had a dalliance with a congregant and I really thought he would marry her. It turned out all she wanted was to be the first lady of a church- any church. Less than three months after he broke things off with her, she married a pastor from a big church in Alexandria. After my heart attack and when Nettie went missing, he made a point of looking after Papi and checking on me. He often came to the house and prayed with us.

I knew he was worried about me, but he kept his questions and his opinions to himself. In the past, he hinted around about wanting to know about Nettie's dad and my marriage. Like everyone else in the church, he was curious about where I went for twenty years and my mysterious return. Unlike others, he never just came out and asked. On some level, for some reason, today I wanted him to ask. I felt like blabbing, but he didn't. It figured. He sat on the corner of my desk while we went over his schedule for the day then went into his office.

I finished my work day without incident and made it to the clinic early. I was tempted to hide in the car until time to see Nettie, but I was exhausted by the idea of trying to avoid Dr. Mercier. Pumping myself up for a confrontation, I smoothed my hair into place and walked to the clinic entrance. After I checked in, I had to wait for a bit since I was so early.

Sitting there, I had time to think about why I was so reluctant to see Daniel. I found myself absently rubbing my stomach though my clothes. When I recognized what I was doing, I snatched my hand away, horrified. I thought I'd put that habit away years ago. Standing, I resisted the urge to pace by studying one of the paintings. Today I planned to tell Nettie about my wedding. It was one of the last truly happy memories I had with Daniel.

When it was finally time for me to go back, I was ready to spill. As usual, she was sitting with her feet tucked under her bottom, staring blankly out the window. At another time in our lives, I would have climbed in bed beside her and wrapped my arms around her. We would have looked out the window together and she would have impressed me by citing the scientific name of any animal or plant in her line of sight. She was always showing off that way. I loved it because it reminded me of her father. The only thing he loved more than learning new things was showing them off.

On our first date, he insisted on wowing me with his knowledge of the history of the saxophone. He must have talked for fifteen minutes straight. I was duly impressed so he kept regaling me with random facts about music and art. It seemed like he was in love with talking, but I didn't mind. I found his voice enthralling.

"Nettie, I brought a picture for you. It's from our wedding. You don't have to look at it right now if you don't feel like it. I'll just leave it on your night stand. Your father and I married on a Tuesday. We wanted to keep things simple, so the only people there were his father, Paulette, and Holly. As a gift, Paulette and Holly pitched in and paid for the pictures and the reception dinner. We had quite a time finding a wedding dress that the three of us could agree on. Even though they knew I was going for elegant and unassuming, the two of them caught wedding fever and tried to rope me into wearing what I like to call a cathedral sized catastrophe! Eventually I put my foot down and selected a white, sleeveless, ankle length dress that looked and felt amazing.

"The ceremony was held on the stretch of beach behind my house at sunset. He wanted the waves licking our feet and the gulls singing songs to us. We wrote our own vows and danced to music that existed in our minds. Daniel made me feel like the most beautiful woman the Lord ever created and I felt like the most blessed woman on earth. They had a caterer come to the house and we were served by waiters in gloves and tuxes. My home was filled with laughter and music. After everyone left, we went back to the beach, sat on the dunes and watched the sun rise. His father paid for our honeymoon cruise. The picture of Daniel on the mantle at the house was taken on our wedding day. Even now, I get choked up when I look at it too long.

"At one point I considered calling Papi, but ultimately I decided not to risk spoiling the day. I wanted both of my parents to share in my happiness. Who wouldn't have? I suppose every little girl dreams of having her mother pray and cajole her through wedding day jitters. It's all but written in stone that a father is expected to walk his precious jewel down the aisle and give her away. Putting those fantasies aside, I knew that the time for repairing such monstrous breaches in both parental relationships was not just before my wedding. In lieu of my parents, I leaned on my friends and my future father-in-law.

"Daniel moved in with me the week after we returned from Barbados and he got a job as the Minister of music at one of the larger churches in the city. I changed my membership to be closer to him.

"He loved his job and seemed to thrive on the choir's performance from week to week. They only rehearsed once a week, but he spent most of the days between writing and preparing new music and arrangements. Our first year was typical for newlyweds. We had a hiccup here and there, but nothing that in my limited experience raised any alarm bells. The only thing I found to be a little strange was the fact that my father-in-law called a lot. He'd call and talk to Daniel at least twice a day and then at some point he'd call and talk to me when Daniel wasn't around. He wanted to know if things were alright. I wondered why he didn't just talk to us both at the same time, but I dismissed my concerns.

"I found out the hard way your father was a spender, where I was a saver. The first time he went on one of his little shopping sprees, he spent something like two thousand dollars in one weekend. I was horrified. I knew he had his own money, but it just seemed so wasteful. Also, I felt as though spending such a large amount of money was something we should have discussed. He was contrite, we moved past it, and that was that.

"Another thing I remember about your father was how he was always intense and in the moment about whatever he was doing. I could come into a room, speak to him, or bring him food and it was entirely possible he would never look up from his keyboard or his notes. He had a tendency to be hyper-focused sometimes, but I thought all creative people were quirky that way.

"Six months into the marriage, I noticed he was sleeping a little less. I'd get up at two or three in the morning and find him sitting at his keyboard with his headphones on. There would be crumbled up paper and sheet music all around him and half empty glasses, soda cans, and water bottles everywhere. When he'd finally notice me standing in the doorway, he'd jump up from his music bench and sweep me into his arms. He'd always say the same thing.

"Vivi, sweet Vivi! My beautiful muse. Make love to me so I can make music the world will love."

"We'd tumble into the bedroom, make love and I'd fall asleep in his arms. Often, I'd get up in the morning and find him back at the keyboard playing, writing, or singing softly to himself. I chalked it all up to art and told myself he'd sleep if he was tired. I was his wife, not his mother. He was too old to have a 'bedtime'.

"One of the last good things I remember about our marriage happened on our first anniversary. I'd planned to make a special dinner, but I never got around to it. Daniel had choir rehearsal that evening and had spent the day at church working up to rehearsal. When he came home I was sitting on the deck watching the waves crash along the shore. The temperature had dropped at sunset, but I hadn't noticed. Wrapping his arms around me, he laid a bouquet of lilies in my lap.

"Vivi, why are you trying to make caramel ice cream out of yourself, woman?"

"Startled, I blurted the first thing that came to mind.

"Daniel, we're pregnant."

"I'd been feeling weak and weepy the past few weeks and it occurred to me that pregnancy was a possibility. We'd often discussed starting a family, but hadn't made any firm plans. I confirmed with my doctor earlier in the afternoon, came home and sat out on the deck to contemplate how to share the news. I'd tried a hundred ways to say it and rejected them all. I hadn't planned to just blurt it out, but I did. I was terrified of his reaction. He'd been working and writing a lot and we were starting to miss time together. He was sleeping at odd times of day and night, exhausted from his irregular hours and I was busier than ever with my business.

"Gathering my courage, I looked into his eyes. Much to my surprise, he had tears running down his face. He placed a trembling hand on my belly. I placed my hand on top of his. Without words, we both shared the same thought, bowed our heads and he began to pray. As he finished his prayer, he stood, swept me into the air, and let out a loud whoop. Setting me back on my feet, he grabbed my hands and like two little kids, we ran to the water below. We dance in the waves laughing and crying. Back in the house we showered together and for the first time in months, we went to sleep together and woke up the same way.

# CHAPTER 10

I kept looking at Nettie hoping for a response, however small. My heart was so full at the memory of being pregnant and happy. I felt if anything could reach her, my joy over sharing the news would have done it. She was still in the same position, but her blinking seemed to increase. Holding my breath, I was afraid to talk and afraid to stop talking.

Encouraged, I decided to keep talking. Sadly I knew what happened next, but that was the point of this whole conversation, wasn't it? Our story took a terrible turn after the announcement. There was no outright nosedive; it was more of a steady slide down a slippery slope. Daniel's descent was persistent and irreversible. For us there was no happy ending. All that aside, for the first time since I'd started my story, I felt like I had her attention.

The glimmer in her eyes told me not only could she hear me, she was listening. I wasn't ready to see the glimmer gone and it was a certain thing that once she heard the rest of what I had to say, the glimmer would leave. Taking a deep breath, I plowed on. Putting this off was no good for either of us.

"The first few months of my pregnancy couldn't have gone better. Daniel was so attentive. He went to the first appointment and they did an ultrasound image. We saw your heartbeat and Daniel decided to call you his little peanut. Seeing you there in black and white made everything real. Again, I wanted to reach out to Papi, but I chickened out. In my own selfish way, I wanted to keep our budding family to myself.

"Because of my age, I was considered a high risk pregnancy. For the first few months I had no real restrictions so other than more frequent doctor visits, I kept my regular schedule. I worked in the Dean's office, I worked on my miniatures and I sketched. I thought about the little family I left with Papi, and tried to imagine what you would look like.

"As my body changed, I drew and created miniatures of myself and my growing belly. I thought maybe when you were older, I'd give them to you. I was in love with the outward manifestation of new life growing inside me. I worried Daniel would find me unattractive, but nothing could have been farther from the truth. He was obsessed with my belly and obsessed with you. We decided to let your gender be a surprise.

"Daniel was the most attentive expectant father! He lavished me with love and attention. He checked on me frequently throughout the day and held me gently during the night. He was so eager to experience the pregnancy and be in each moment with me. I loved it. He made me feel so cherished.

"As much as he loved on me and showered me with attention, he doted on you. Once I began to show, he would throw himself across the bed at your 'bedtime' to tell you a story and to sing your special bedtime song. He sat up and wrote it the night I told him about you. Daniel's voice was deep, strong, and smooth. It always seemed odd to hear him crooning a lullaby, but it became a nightly ritual for us.

"I've never forgotten the words to your lullaby even after all these years.

*'Sweet little baby all wrapped in love, tiniest angel, our gift from above.*

*Covered by His blood, saved by His grace,*

*Lord I can't wait to see your little face.*

*Oh my angel, oh my angel, swaddled with love from the start,*

*Oh my angel, oh my angel, you hold the key to my heart!*

"Each night, as he did his thing, I felt like I was getting a glimpse of what our future held. There was music, laughter, and love. Nettie, I wish I could tell you it stayed that way, but clearly it didn't. As sweet as your father was being to me, he was changing in other areas of his life, and not for the better. At the time, I excused the changes away because of your impending birth. I'd read somewhere men had a tendency to freak out as pregnancy progressed.

"When I was about six months along, Daniel stopped keeping his regular work schedule. He stopped attending rehearsals and stopped writing. More often than not, he wanted to stay home with me. I thought he was being ridiculous, but he wouldn't budge. He said he was terrified of me needing him and not being available to me. I let it go because on some level, it was nice to know he was making things about me and catering to me. I wasn't used to him being clingy, but I didn't want to examine it too closely.

"He began to insist on driving me everywhere. Even though my stomach wasn't protruding much at all, he made a point of pushing the passenger seat in the car as far back as it could go. I decided he was just being overly cautious. One afternoon he demanded I sit in the back seat all together. I flatly refused. It was the first time we'd ever really argued. Up until that point, he'd never even raised his voice to me.

"That day, he yelled, screamed, and stomped around the house. He knocked over tables, chairs, his keyboard, and my easels. He called me selfish and irresponsible. It was awful. The more he yelled the more quiet I became. I'd never seen him act that way. Even when we disagreed about something, there were no vocal outbursts. Part of me was just incredulous that all the drama was about me sitting in the back of the car. I wasn't afraid he would hurt me physically, but my feelings were hurt. Unsure how to handle the confrontation and the violence, I burst into tears. We both apologized, and I ended up doing things his way to keep down confusion. He cleaned up the mess and just like when he spent all that money, we moved on.

"I felt his response was a little dramatic, but in the end, I convinced myself he was just overzealous about my safety. Because I couldn't reconcile his behavior with the loving husband he'd been, I ignored what I didn't want to see. It really is amazing what behavior people can convince themselves to accept. I should have called Mr. McCarvey. I could have put him out. I could have left him. Instead, I chose to 'stay in love'.

"The strangest thing was when he started touching my belly constantly. At the beginning it was like he was cradling you. I loved it. He mostly did it at home when it was just the two of us. As my body continued to change, so did he. His touch changed from loving and affectionate, to protective, but in a weird way. It was like he was obsessed with my belly. He was beginning to make a nuisance of himself and I had no idea how to address it.

"Nettie, hindsight being what it is, I now realize your father's behavior wasn't in any way normal. I also realize I wasn't the only person who recognized something was wrong. His father's calls became constant. I didn't want to acknowledge my intuition, and Mr. McCarvey didn't want to be right about his suspicions. He could have done us all a favor and come clean, but as the saying goes, 'Coulda, shoulda, woulda, never did.'

"The warning signs were all there. Daniel was losing his grip on reality. When he first started talking to you, his tone was happy, playful and light. He'd ask you silly questions like if you'd like us to decorate your nursery with giraffes or dolphins. He wanted to know if you thought it was too soon for him to buy your first bike.

"In the last few weeks before everything exploded, his tone was more serious and secretive. Instead of curling up next to my stomach, he started hiding his head under the covers to talk to you. He whispered. One night I heard him say he was worried about you. He asked you if you thought you had enough room.

"I wasn't sure what to think about that. Earlier we'd gone to the doctor. At that point in my pregnancy, during each visit, the nurse would measure my stomach and check your growth. The last few times there hadn't been much change, but we'd been told it was nothing to be concerned about. While I was content not to become a blimp, Daniel was worried you'd run out of space to grow. I didn't want to, but I had to ask him what he meant.

"For the second time in our marriage, Daniel yelled at me and for the first time I could remember, he called me by my given name.

"Vivianne, I wasn't talking to you, but since you want to butt in, this is your fault! I bring you food. I rub oil on your belly. I pray for our baby, but you won't make room. You are squishing our baby. You're too little. TOO LITTLE!"

"He jumped off the bed and ran out of the room. Scared and confused, I followed him into the kitchen. He was mumbling and ranting, slinging drawers open and slamming them shut. I wanted to calm him down, but I didn't know how or where to start.

"Daniel, baby. You need to calm down. You're making a mess and you're scaring me," I said. I was trying to make eye contact with him, but I was afraid to get too close. I'd never had a reason to worry about him hurting me, but at that moment, some part of me was braced for a physical attack.

"You should be scared, you murderer! You're killing our baby!" His eyes were wild and the veins on his neck bulged. Sweat stains had formed around the collar and at the arm pits of his shirt.

"What? Daniel, what the hell is wrong with you?

"By this time, he'd found what he was looking for. I saw his hand close on a knife from the butcher's block, but my brain refused to process the information. I'd unknowingly backed myself into a corner in the dining room and there was nowhere for me to run. Daniel dropped to his knees and knife in hand, he crawled to me. His eyes were red from crying and he was drenched in sweat. He stopped inches from me and instead of talking to me, he began to sing your lullaby.

*'Sweet little baby all wrapped in love, tiniest angel, our gift from above.*

*Covered by His blood, saved by His grace,*

*Lord I can't wait to see your little face.*

*Oh my angel, oh my angel, swaddled with love from the start,*

*Oh my angel, oh my angel, you hold the key to my heart!*

"The love in his voice stood in stark contrast to the crazed look on his face. With his left hand he reached out and cradled the side of my stomach. I was terrified. Nettie, I wish I could tell you I fought him tooth and nail. That some sort of maternal instinct took over and pumped me full of adrenaline, allowing me to overpower him and save myself. The truth is, I was so confused and afraid, I just stood there. He stopped singing and started whispering to you again. He promised to save you. He told you he had a plan to make room for you so you could grow again.

"I was sure I would die that night. As he calmly slashed the knife across my belly, I prayed for all of us, but for you most of all. I was only seven months along and I couldn't bear the thought of you suffering. I prayed a swift death for us all, as I was sure when Daniel realized what he had done, his end would be next. I prayed for Papi, because I knew finding out I'd had a family and he'd lost us all in one swoop would break him if he wasn't already broken. I prayed hardest for Mr. McCarvey. He would feel the loss more than anyone. As I slumped onto the floor, I saw his face outside the patio door. I remember being embarrassed that my father-in-law had come by when there was so much blood on the floor. It was a ridiculous thing to worry about, but numb and cold, I closed my eyes and floated away."

# CHAPTER 11

She moved. Nettie was standing next to me. I was so caught up in the horror of the end of my marriage, I didn't notice her get up from the bed and come to me. Her eyes were clear, but full to the brim with tears. She'd heard me. I wanted to reach for her, but I didn't dare. What if she went away again? I was terrified of pushing her too hard and I was completely raw from what I'd just shared.

Other than what had to be told to the police and the emergency room staff, I'd never said more than a sentence or two here and there about that night. Not to Paulette, not to Holly, and certainly not to Papi. Unsure of what to do next, I kept talking. She may as well hear the rest of the story. As far as I was concerned, the next part was the part that counted anyway.

"Clearly, my injury wasn't fatal. As it turned out, Mr. McCarvey had been trying to reach us for two days. I didn't realize it, but Daniel had unplugged the phones. This was before everybody had a cell phone glued to their hip. When he couldn't reach us, he booked a flight and raced over. He used a patio chair to break into the house and he tackled Daniel. He was able to keep him subdued while he called 911 and then he called their lawyer.

"Nettie, this is the part that makes me mad even now. He knew. From the moment he met me, he knew Daniel wasn't well and he knew Daniel hadn't told me. I'd been in the hospital for two days before he came to see me. Apparently his first priority was making sure Daniel stayed out of jail. If I sound bitter about it, then I'm sorry. I know I've never mentioned another grandparent to you, but there is a reason for it.

"He came in my room with a little teddy bear and sat in the chair next to my bed. So many years later and I still remember every word he said.

"He started with a lame apology. 'Vivianne, I guess I owe you an apology. I was an ignorant fool and it almost got you killed. You see, my son is sick. He's brain sick. He gets it from his Mama and she got it from her Pa. I didn't want it, you see, so I made excuses for him. When he was nine, he had it bad. His Mama had been doing fine, but then she got pregnant again. She was worried about losing her figure so she started wearing a corset. She slept in it and even bathed in it. The baby couldn't grow. Daniel was home with her when she finally miscarried. She refused to call for help and he watched her bleed to death. Right at the end, she finally begged him to save the baby by cutting the corset off. By the time I got home, both she and the baby were dead. I tried to take care of Daniel on my own. I did my best, you have to believe me.

"I found he had a musical talent and I just poured everything into that. When he was in high school, I did take him to a doctor. She said he needed therapy and medicine for the rest of his life. I was fine with a pill if that was all, but I don't believe in all the shrink mumbo jumbo. If he needed somebody to talk to, I figured he could talk to me. For a long time it worked. He talked to me and he took his medicine. When you came into his life, I thought he'd talk to you, but he didn't. He was afraid to lose you. When he found out you were pregnant, I knew it was only a matter of time before something went wrong. I figured out a few weeks ago he was off his meds. I know I should have told you. I could have saved us all a bunch of heartache. I know sorry won't fix it, but you have to understand. He's my son.'

"As I lay there all bandaged up listening to him talk I was literally drowning in grief. I was alive but my little family was dead. There was no way for us to survive this. There was no reality I could imagine where we would be able to reconcile. My marriage was over in less than two years. He reached into his jacket and pulled out two envelopes. His next words effectively ended our relationship."

"He said, 'No amount of money will fix this. At this point all you and I can do is salvage things for Daniel. Jail is not where he belongs. Surly you know that. The baby is going to be fine and so will you. I spoke with the family attorney and the DA's office. Because I can prove he's had issues in the past, we can get this all squared away with a little time in a hospital back home in Ohio. Because you two are married, I can't do it. You have to. As his wife, you are responsible for him. If I can get you to sign this, we can get his transfer started. I want you to have the best care and everything, so in the other envelope you'll find a substantial peace offering. I know this is a lot to think about so I'll leave you here and give you some time to think things over.'

# CHAPTER 12

"What a jackass!"

Nettie's voice was rough and husky. It reminded me of my own. I held my breath, waiting to hear more. Slowly, as not to startle her, I reached out to her with a trembling hand. I'd waited years for this moment. There was no way to stop myself from taking what I needed. A hug. At first, she was stiff in my arms, but after a moment something shifted. She hugged me back. We poured so much into that moment.

Touching her again was surreal. I tried to take the moment piece by piece. I tried to gobble it up all at once. I tried to somehow freeze it and preserve it. Her hair, her skin, the way she smelled. Every imaginable sensation assaulted me, and I thanked God for it.

Holding her in my arms again erased so much pain. It reminded me of the phenomena old people called labor amnesia. So much blood, sweat, tears, and prayer go into having a baby. There's pain, fear, and uncertainty. All of it erased at the sound of the child's first cry. With a single embrace, all the pain of the last twenty or more years was swept away. The misery and isolation that cloaked me when she was missing dissolved like mist in sunshine with the sound of her voice. If she never spoke again, I thanked God for those three words.

Tears ran freely down both our faces. I pulled back to look into her eyes. They were bright and shiny with awareness, her lashes spiky. Smiling I wiped her cheeks. "Yes, baby. What a jackass!"

Laughing, she placed her palms on my face. "Mama I love you, but you sound funny cussing."

I shook my head at our nonsensical conversation. She grabbed my hand and led me to her bed. We sat there for a while and said nothing. I knew I'd have to leave soon, but I didn't want to. The idea of leaving her hurt me. What if she was back inside her head when I came back? I could lose her again. She seemed to know what I was thinking. Clearing her throat, her voice came out as a throaty whisper.

"Mama, I know something isn't right with me. I know I've been lost somewhere in my head. I liked it there for a while because I thought I did bad things. I kind of came back to myself the first night you were here. I read your letters. I should have said something, but I was afraid. I couldn't keep disappointing you. I know we need to talk and I know you have more to say. Maybe you can come back tomorrow?"

It's like she knew exactly what I needed to hear. Squeezing her hand gently, I said, "Nothing can keep me from it. I love you, Nettie. You'll always be my little chocolate china doll."

Reluctantly, I pushed the button to buzz me out of the room. Once in the hallway, I wasn't sure what to do. Was I supposed to tell someone she was talking? Selfishness made me keep it to myself. She talked to me. That didn't mean she was ready to talk to the world.

Getting into my car, I headed home. As grateful as I was, we still had more hurdles to cross in our talk. What happened to Daniel?

Why did I move back to Louisiana? How did Papi turn into Grandy? I'd lived and died a thousand times over the past two decades. I was exhausted both mentally and physically.

I used the drive home to gather my thoughts. While waiting at a red light, I caught a glimpse of myself in the rear view mirror. There were bags under my eyes. My skin had a dull cast to it and my bun was neither smooth nor sleek. I looked as bad as I felt. Stressed or not, if Nettie and I were to survive this phase of our lives, I was going to have to get some sleep. The last thing I needed was another heart attack. The plan was eat, shower, pray, sleep.

Well, we all know what happens when we make plans. By the time I made it home, Papi was already in bed. I check the clock in the kitchen and saw it was barely seven. Now who was avoiding who? Shaking my head, I went to my room to put my things away and slip on my house shoes.

On my desk, I saw a thick cream colored envelope. Curious, I opened it. I stopped reading after the first page. I didn't know what to say, what to think, or how to feel. The timing of it all was ironic. Mr. McCarvey was dead. He'd left everything to me. I knew he was well off, but I had no concept of how deep his pockets were. My knee jerk reaction was to reject anything to do with him, but as tired as I was I couldn't think straight.

My appetite gone, I showered and dressed for bed. Settling down on my knees, I began to pray. My bedtime prayer should have been jubilant, but I sounded weary. I wanted to feel like Shouting John, but I didn't. I just felt beat up. Feeling like an ungrateful hypocrite, I climbed into bed and prepared myself for a fitful night of tossing and turning. I thought I'd have trouble sleeping, but I surprised myself by dozing off as soon as my head hit the pillow. For the first time in forever, my sleep was dreamless and I was thankful for it.

When I got up the next morning, Papi was gone. I wondered where he could be heading so early and I decided to make a point of getting home in time to at least have dinner with him. Rev. Harvey had multiple counseling appointments scheduled for the day as well as a class to teach. I was eager to get to work and get started with my day. Since I'd skipped dinner the night before I was starving. I'd just sat down to eat when the phone rang. Looking at the caller ID, I recognized the number for Waterview. My stomach dropped. Something must be wrong with Nettie! Panicked, I snatched the phone from its cradle, expecting to hear bad news.

"Mrs. McCarvey, this is Samantha. I'm Dr. Mercier's secretary. She'd like to set a time to see you as soon as possible."

My brain did a few swift calculations. If something was going on with Nettie, she would have said so. Telling me to set a time to come in meant this was about Daniel. While I'd known this was coming, I still wasn't ready. I wasn't interested in Daniel, just Nettie. Over the years I'd managed to avoid or decline these requests, but during that time, I wasn't visiting the clinic everyday either. By running out of the clinic the other day, I'd just been putting off the inevitable. Now, I refused to delude myself about the reason for her persistence. I decided these requests definitely weren't about Nettie, especially given the letter sitting on my desk. Mr. McCarvey was Daniel's primary contact. With him gone, once again, Daniel's future was in my hands.

Putting this off was not going to make it go away, so I agreed to make time for Dr. Mercier after I saw Nettie. I needed to see her 'alive' again before I could make a fair decision where her dad was concerned. Hanging up the phone with a sigh, I saw my breakfast was cold. Feeling defeated, I trudged back to my room, grabbed my things, including the letter and headed to work.

My work day was as hectic as I predicted, but I made it through. Finishing on time, I stopped to look at the mural in the sanctuary on my way out. Papi was right about what it represented, and today I was going to have to press to make progress, too. I'd taken the time to read the attorney's entire letter during my lunch break. It was as I thought. Because Daniel and I never divorced and because he was considered mentally incompetent, all of Mr. McCarvey's assets now belonged to me. I was still responsible for Daniel and there was a possibility I could have him home with me.

Telling Nettie our love story confirmed I still loved him. My dreams each night told me he still meant something to me. Was there a chance that after all this time I could resurrect my little family? My heart said maybe, the scars on my stomach said never.

There was a reason I chose to stay married, but single. I knew what I had with Daniel, as complicated as it was, was all I ever wanted. Our laughter, his music, my art, our lovemaking- that combination could never be duplicated. If I couldn't have that, I'd rather have nothing. He should have told me about himself. We may have been able to withstand the perils of mental illness together. God knew I loved him enough to try. I just wish Daniel had known it, too. The question now, was did I still love him enough to try?

After so much time, I realized I was still tired of being alone. I mourned my lost marriage every day. I comforted myself with Daniel's laughter and kept his music in my heart. For years, I was ashamed of myself for continuing to love him. I'd almost convinced myself I didn't. I refused to go see him. I wouldn't respond to his letters or any communication from his therapists. In the light of day I turned my heart to stone where he was concerned, but at night things were different. My soul cried out for him. I'd suffered panic attacks for years. Not because he hurt me, but because he hurt me and I still loved him.

Twenty-two years ago I couldn't get past the physical hurt long enough to entertain any healing or reconciliation. The fear was crippling. What would people say? How could I love a man who sliced me open from hip to hip? Maybe we were both crazy. When I decided to come back to Lampling, I had a baby to consider. Hell, I still had a baby to consider.

There was also a sense of betrayal because of how his father handled things. I never got over how callus he was, sitting in my hospital room with his blood money. I couldn't understand how he could be so heartless, concerned only about Daniel and the family reputation. Clearly he was no longer a consideration. No matter what, I had a lot to think about.

Deciding I'd procrastinated long enough, I locked up the church and headed to Waterview. Again.

# CHAPTER 13

I don't know what I expected when I signed in. Balloons? A banner screaming Nettie's recovery? Everything was the same as the day before. I was led back to Nettie's room and my heart dropped to the floor. She was on her bed with her feet tucked under her bottom, looking out the window at nothing. I wanted to die. My feet were glued to the floor and my tongue clung to the roof of my mouth. My throat clogged with tears. I'd known better than to get my hopes up, but I did it anyway. Now what?

"Hey, Mama."

Two more words. They were all I'd prayed for and more than I'd hoped to receive. Another gift from God. Struggling to speak around my tears, I managed a, "Hi," in return. My legs threatened to give out on me so I forced one foot in front of the other, making it over to my little stool.

"Are you going to tell me the rest?"

Clearing my throat, I managed a, "Yes". She still hadn't turned around from the window, but at least she was talking. She knew I was there and she wanted to know more. Digging deep, I gave it to her.

"My decision to move back to Louisiana was a difficult one. I knew by coming home, I was effectively shutting doors that would probably never be opened again. I had no idea if Papi would take me back and allow me to be myself, but I also felt like maybe letting him pull my strings again would be okay even if just for a little while. I was reluctant to lose my independence, but what had my rebellion gotten me?

I refused to sign Mr. McCarvey's papers. I didn't want anything to do with him. As far as I was concerned, my injuries were as much his fault as Daniel's. He should have said something, and trying to save face after the fact was despicable. When I was well enough to leave the hospital, I got in my car and drove to Lampling. I needed my Papi and if he would have me, I was going home.

I showed up on his doorstep married, pregnant, and terrified. He opened his arms and it was like I never left. We'd both changed and we were the same. He relished the opportunity to rescue me and I was glad to let him.

"He drove back to Florida with me to help me pack my things, sell my house, and close my business. With his help, we had Daniel committed and transferred to Louisiana. He was there for me when you were born. He helped me raise you. When you started showing signs of being different, I was scared. I should have tried to help you, but I fell into the same cycle of denial Mr. McCarvey did. No one wants to deal with the reality of mental illness, but ignoring it doesn't make it go away.

"I did exactly what he did, only worse. At least he got medication for Daniel. I didn't even do that much. I was afraid to acknowledge your issues because if I did, that made them real. I wanted a different life for you, so I let you leave. I called frequently to see if you were okay. I prayed over you daily and when I couldn't reach you, I showed up on your doorstep. Now, here we are. All of us. Your father is here, Nettie. He's been in Waterview all along."

I waited. She sat. I stood again and began to pace. I thought the silence would be uncomfortable, but it wasn't. After so many years of keeping things bottled up, there was a feeling of liberation now that it was all said. I was just about to give up on her speaking again, when I saw her move from the corner of my eye.

Turning around to face her, I realized she was different. Her eyes were alert and bright and her skin no longer looked dull. Her nails and cuticles were smooth and filed where the day before they'd been ragged. She looked rested instead of haunted. She turned to put her feet on the floor and reached for me. Her effort was all I needed. I launched myself at her and sat next to her on the bed.

"Mama, I get it. A little. What a mess right? I got a chance to talk to Dr. Ruth last night. She's been worried about me. She didn't say it, but I think she was worried about you too. I don't want you to think you did anything wrong. You didn't. You did your best and now since we know the truth, we can both do better.

"I'm schizophrenic. There, I said it and

the roof didn't fall on our heads. It's not a reflection on you and it's no one's fault. I know I can have a good life with help. That means medicine and therapy, not just prayer. I still feel like I shouldn't be around people yet, so if it's okay with you, Dr. Ruth and I think I should stay here a while longer. I think I may want to meet Daniel someday too, if that's okay with you. If you don't want me to, I won't."

Now it was my turn to be overwhelmed. There was a sense of relief because I wasn't being forced to make her stay. There was fear because I didn't know what to do about her meeting Daniel. On the way over here, I was thinking I might be ready to see him, but bringing them together was a jump.

I wondered if he even wanted to see me. So much had happened. I was willing to acknowledge to myself I'd never stopped loving him, but was the feeling mutual? There was a point years ago when he wrote me daily. I returned each letter unopened. Had too much time passed? More than anything, I wished for a set of circumstances where we could at least be in the same room together. I missed him.

Behind me the door clicked. It was

Nettie's aide. Glancing at my watch I saw it was time for my meeting with Dr. Mercier. Giving her hands a light squeeze, I stood up. I wanted to say something, but she didn't seem interested in a response. As I left the room, she went back to her spot by the window.

As we retraced our path back toward the front of the building, for the first time I heard evidence of other residents. Curious, I asked about it. The aide turned us left instead of right and led me to what appeared to be a community activity room. It was like walking into a spacious play room or den. There were over-sized chairs and small end tables scattered throughout the room. There was what appeared to be a designated crafting area. Calling the room cheerful may have been a stretch, but it did have positive energy.

By the window some of the residents and their visitors were gathered around a man playing a brown upright piano. I didn't have to walk into the room to know it was him. I could see his profile. He took my breath away. He was still the most handsome man I'd ever seen. My heart was in my throat and I couldn't move. After all these years, my response to him was still just as strong as it was the day we met. I'd been a fool for trying to deny my deep, abiding love for this man.

I was so shaken by the reality of seeing him again, it took me a moment to realize not only was he playing, someone was singing. Her voice was deep, smooth and sultry. All I could see was her back and all I heard was Nettie's lullaby. Even though I'd not heard it in more than sixty years, I recognized my Mama's voice.

# CHAPTER 14

Dr. Mercier was talking to me. At first she sounded far away, but as I looked to my left, she was there beside me. I allowed her to take me by the hand and lead me to her office. Minutes went by with neither of us speaking. What was there to say? I figured I'd let her go first however long it took. She looked as uncomfortable as I felt, so I guess that was something.

"Mrs. McCarvey, I'm sure you've had quite a shock today. May I get you some water?"

"No. Water is the last thing I'd like. What would do me some good right now is an answer. How long has she been coming here? If you can tell me, I'd appreciate it."

There was no need to pretend we didn't know who 'she' was. She was singing with

Daniel. She was familiar enough with him to know Nettie's lullaby. She looked enough like me that anyone with eyes could have made the connection.

"Fifteen years, twice a week. More since his father has been deceased. He's been doing well, by the way. I know the two of you have a complex situation, but when you're ready to talk about it, we can. He's made tremendous progress over the years. We believe he is capable of living outside of this facility with supervision and I think at some point you should consider it.

"He's indicated recently he'd like to speak with you, and from a therapeutic point of view, I think he should. As for Mrs. Fontenot's visits, I can only say having someone who looked so much like you come to see him really seemed to help him reconnect with reality. Where he was unable to communicate with you by letter, he's been able to sort of practice talking things out with her. It really is remarkable how much the two of you favor. I know all of this is a bit unorthodox, but it has helped in ways I never could have imagined.

"It's strange how the world works. You would never have come here if things hadn't gone so poorly with your daughter. I know you're probably upset with me right now. I'm fine with that, but I will ask you to consider what has been gained this week. Your mother and your husband are down the hall. You can talk to them or you can walk away. Your choice. There's no judgment here. She usually leaves by six and he always goes back to his room after that. I can have someone take you to him if you like."

She made it all sound so simple. Go see him and say what? *Daniel, I'm sorry I had to have you locked up for the last twenty years. Hey, let's pick up where we left off! While you were gone we had a daughter and I messed her up worse than you. She's got a room here, too. By the way I'm still in love with you.*

What was he supposed to say to me? *I'm sorry, Vivi. I should have told you I was slap-assed crazy. Sorry I had a psychotic break and tried to carve our baby out of you. Sorry my dad tried to cover it up by throwing money at you. Thanks for coming by.*

The whole thing was awful. Dr. Mercier was waiting for a decision. She said she wasn't going to judge me, but her scrutiny was palpable. For some reason her opinion mattered to me. I didn't want her to think I was some horrible person who'd locked her husband in a loony bin and thrown away the key. I wanted to scream at the unfairness of it all. Instead of shrieking like a mad woman, I stood and adopted a demeanor Papi would have been proud of. With a voice that belied my inner turmoil, I said, "I'll see him."

Three life changing words. I was taken down a second hallway and led to a room identical to Nettie's. Daniel was sitting on his bed looking out the window at nothing. As the door clicked shut behind me I was embraced by Cool Water. I closed my eyes and for a moment I was at my desk in Dean Jackson's office again. I opened them to find him standing in front of me.

He was still tall. He still oozed confidence and charm. His ebony skin still begged to be touched. I had to command my hands to stay by my sides. I thought I would be afraid to be alone with him, yet I only felt relief. My body came alive, my heart pounding, my palms sweating, my stomach full of butterflies. When he spoke, I was mesmerized. I couldn't have moved or spoken if my life had depended on it.

"Vivi, you came. Thank you. I want you to know I will fix this. I want you and I want our marriage. Maybe that makes me a fool. I'm fine with being a fool for you. If it takes the rest of my natural born days, I will earn your love again. I've been praying for eight thousand ninety five days for the chance to say this to your face. I should have trusted your love for me enough to tell you I was sick. By allowing my fear of losing you to make decisions for me, I lost you anyway. If you never want to see me again I understand.

"In a perfect world you'd let me court you again. You'd introduce me to our child and we could have that little family you wanted. I never stopped loving you even when I didn't love myself. I know it may be asking a lot for you to still love me, but if you could at least allow me to be your friend, I would be grateful."

His voice was still deep. It rumbled through me like an earthquake. Never in a million years could I have foretold this conversation. True, I'd never been able to predict what Daniel would say, but this took the cake. I wanted nothing more than to fall into his arms and pick up where we left off, minus the stabbing. I wanted his love. I wanted the happily ever after. I did want my little family, but this was all too much.

How insane was this? My brain was cramping, trying to swallow this new reality.

Nettie was safe, Daniel was sane again, and my long lost mother was back? Why not? It was just too much. I felt a panic attack coming on. I needed to get out. I was about to push the buzzer, when I felt a hand on my hip.

Falling back into Daniel's arms was like jumping off a cliff. Fast, exciting, exhilarating, and possibly the dumbest thing I'd ever done. Calling myself all kinds of idiot, I welcomed his embrace. Turning to face him, I looked into his eyes and fell into his soul. Electricity rolled through my body from my lips and tongue. His kiss scorched me inside and out. I'd never allowed myself to entertain the idea of being in his arms again, yet here I was. Trembling in his arms, I was a virgin on my honeymoon again, dancing in the moonlight, ready to follow where he led.

The click of the door behind me shattered the moment. Nettie's aide opened the door and cleared her throat awkwardly. I hastily stepped away from him, but he held my hand as though he couldn't bear to be separated from me for even a moment. Coming back to my senses, I was grateful for the interruption. Belatedly, it occurred to me that there were cameras in the rooms. Embarrassed at the thought of being caught kissing like two horny teenagers, we followed her to Dr. Mercier's office. I tried to take back my hand, but Daniel wasn't having it. For some reason, that made me happy.

Once again I found myself in her brown leather chair, studying the wall behind her desk. We waited in silence, holding hands. I realized I hadn't given him an answer. I had one. I just had no idea how to verbalize it. There was a lot to consider and I needed to approach our issues with equal parts care and prayer. I didn't want to get caught up in an unrealistic fantasy and set myself up for more heartache.

For so long I'd prayed for restoration. I'd sought peace. I'd longed for companionship. Now it appeared to be right in front of me on a silver platter with a huge bank account attached to it. Did I dare? Closing my eyes, my mind returned to the mural at the church again. Faith plus effort. It was time for me to press if I was to have the desire of my heart. I opened my eyes and turned to face Daniel. He'd been staring at me. I could tell. Gathering my courage, I began to speak, my words stilted and stiff at first, soon flowed like spring river water.

"Daniel, I'm going to date you. Not today,

but soon. We will have lunch in the park. We will drive to a lake and watch the sunset. We can sit on a blanket and you can tell me all about yourself and I will tell you all about myself. We can laugh, talk, and maybe hold hands. I love you. I never stopped. I guess at this point, it's safe to say I never will."

When Dr. Mercier finally came to the office, she found us facing each other, on our knees, foreheads touching. We prayed for our marriage, our daughter, and our future. We thanked God for our path, rocky as it had been. I was afraid he would expect me to jump up and pack his things and bring him home. Thankfully, he really meant what he said about doing the work we'd need to restore our relationship. We made arrangements to get counseling together and scheduled time to visit outside the clinic. Our transition was going to be slow and gradual.

We didn't talk about Nettie or Helene. I guess Dr. Mercier figured I had enough going on at the moment. Grateful for her compassion and support, I drove home in a daze. I really wanted to get home and talk to Papi. There was so much to say. So much to share. I realized he didn't even know Nettie was talking again.

When I pulled up to the house, I was glad to see the living room lights on. With a renewed sense of purpose, I bounded up the front steps, opened the front door and dropped my keys in the little bowl by the window.

Papi was sitting in his recliner and Helene was in mine. Well hell. I'd spent the last week digging around an emotional graveyard. Why should I have been surprised to find my dead relationship with Helene resurrected?

# EPILOGUE

As a mother, you have one job. Be an advocate for your child. With a single cry, babies demand priority over your own parents, your husband, even yourself. It's a job many women look forward to even as children themselves. I was no different. I looked forward to the day I could wear the many hats of motherhood. I wanted to look in a mirror and see a provider, and educator, a protector, and a confidante. I was prepared to succeed, too. When a mother succeeds, society benefits. When she fails, the entire world suffers.

I was under the impression a good mother could also manage to have a good marriage and be a good wife. I never expected to have to choose. I've been gone a long time. It seems as though Gerald and I have some explaining to do.

# Full Circle

To Be Released 2017

At last my family was together again. I never thought I would have had Vivianne and Helene sitting in the same room with me. I knew seeing her mother in our living room was a shock to Vivianne and I was sure they were waiting on me to say something, but I had no words.

Searching for the right thing to say, I kept looking at them. Vivianne looked just like her mother. They were the same height, had the same face, the same hair and the same voice. I glanced back and forth between them and it was almost like seeing double.

Not sure what to do, my eyes focused on Helene. She was staring at Vivianne like she'd never seen her before. I took the chance to study her a little. Even in her eighties, she was stunning. Her hair was more silver than black and hung in waves around her face, across her shoulders, and down her back. As usual, I wanted to bury my face in it and as usual, I did no such thing. After all these years, I still found myself fighting for control where she was concerned.

She hadn't said anything yet, but I leaned forward in my chair, waiting for her to break the silence. I loved her voice. There was a story to tell and as I never was a man of many words, I figured she'd be the one to tell our daughter everything.

# ABOUT THE AUTHOR

Originally from Pensacola, Florida, Sonya Ferrell moved to Central Louisiana to settle down and raise her family. In the course of becoming an author, Sonya strayed down many strange and different paths in her search to find who she wanted to be. Her stray paths include being a mortician's assistant, a stand up comedian, a banking officer, an ambulance driver, a massage therapist, a stylist, and a former member of The United States Air Force.

Although, she'd tell you she's no where near where she will be when she's grown up; she would definitely say that she's found another piece of her soul. A soul that is forever searching to find balance with the vivacious, fun, ever-learning, exciting, physical self that is the Author, Sonya Ferrell.

Made in the USA
Charleston, SC
18 October 2016